"Jennifer Eivaz is uniquely qualified to write about the glory of God. She has lived it and transferred it to so many people. I've known her for over twenty years, and I can attest that she brings the glory on a consistent basis. This book will surely help you do the same thing in every context of society. Can you imagine the glory of God infiltrating factories, sports arenas, schools, government and media? This book will surely contribute to this process for the glory of God."

Paul Marc Goulet, senior pastor,
International Church of Las Vegas

"Jennifer describes in plain language aspects of the spiritual realm that are often misunderstood or considered out of reach for the ordinary person, and she passionately challenges each of us to become a glory carrier. We are learning that a lifestyle of signs and wonders is a reflection of our relationship with the Holy Spirit, a relationship many of us have never considered that deeply. Jennifer asks us, 'Do you have an intimate friendship with the Spirit of God?' And then she invites you into the process of transforming in His presence."

Banning Liebscher, founder and pastor, Jesus Culture

"*Glory Carriers* is one of the most profound and comprehensive books that I have read on the topic of glory. Jennifer Eivaz has beautifully written a power-packed book that creates an appetite and environment for the presence of God. Each chapter will equip readers to partner with the Holy Spirit to release signs, wonders and miracles in their everyday life. Jennifer's teachings, stories and Holy Spirit encounters will activate the faith required to receive a 'double portion' mantle of God's glory to fulfill your calling. If you've felt a heavy burden of God on your life, then this book is the answer that you are a heavyweight in the Spirit called to become a glory carrier!"

Hakeem Collins, founder and CEO, Champions
International; author, *Heaven Declares, Prophetic
Breakthrough* and *Command Your Healing*

"*Glory Carriers* is a powerful invitation to go deeper in your relationship with the Spirit of God. Jennifer Eivaz lays a strong biblical foundation for the spiritual truth that every believer in Jesus can be a carrier of God's glory. *Glory Carriers* provides an eye-opening look at the person of the Holy Spirit, which is a foundational key for every Christ follower."

Debbie Kitterman, founder, Dare 2 Hear;
author, *The Gift of Prophetic Encouragement*

"This revelatory book is the cure not only for your spiritual hunger but also for the lack of it. You can know the personality, intelligence, will and feelings of the Holy Spirit as you develop a friendship with Him, and Jennifer is uniquely anointed to help you do just that."

Laura Harris Smith, author, *Seeing the Voice of God*;
host, theTHREE

"The King of glory is coming! We have entered a new era where we shall see the glory of God like we have never seen before. Psalm 24:7–9 says the King of glory is coming 'through you.' *Glory Carriers* is a deep well of wisdom and encouragement that will draw you deeper in intimacy with Him and challenge you to receive His glory in whatever form and way He chooses to come! You will be awakened to greater revelation of who He is and how you reflect Him. You will be left with a sense of awe at the privilege that it is to carry His glory! Awaken Glory Carrier, it's your time!"

Lana Vawser, prophetic voice, author and speaker,
Lana Vawser Ministries

"My great friend Jennifer Eivaz has written a phenomenal book: *Glory Carriers*. I have made this title my lifelong prayer request—this theme is *that* important! This book is sure to provoke new hunger for God's touch on your life and influence your impact on the world around you. You need to read this!"

Sean Smith, founder, Pointblank International;
author, *Prophetic Evangelism* and *I Am Your Sign*

GLORY
CARRIERS

GLORY
CARRIERS

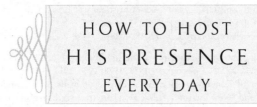

HOW TO HOST
HIS PRESENCE
EVERY DAY

JENNIFER EIVAZ

Chosen

a division of Baker Publishing Group
Minneapolis, Minnesota

© 2019 by Jennifer Eivaz

Published by Chosen Books
11400 Hampshire Avenue South
Bloomington, Minnesota 55438
www.chosenbooks.com

Chosen Books is a division of
Baker Publishing Group, Grand Rapids, Michigan

Printed in the United States of America

ISBN 978-0-8007-9855-0

Library of Congress Cataloging-in-Publication Data
Names: Eivaz, Jennifer, author.
Title: Glory carriers : how to host His presence every day / Jennifer Eivaz.
Description: Minneapolis : Chosen, a division of Baker Publishing Group, 2019. |
    Includes bibliographical references.
Identifiers: LCCN 2018040984| ISBN 9780800798550 (pbk.) | ISBN 9781493417384
    (e-book)
Subjects: LCSH: Holy Spirit. | Glory of God—Christianity. | Christian life.
Classification: LCC BT123 .E38 2019 | DDC 231.7—dc23
LC record available at https://lccn.loc.gov/2018040984

Cover design by Rob Williams, InsideOutCreativeArts

19 20 21 22 23 24 25   8 7 6 5 4 3 2

green
press
INITIATIVE

I dedicate this book to the Holy Spirit,
my fierce and gentle Friend,
who never fails to surprise me
with something new and something more.

Contents

Foreword

In her new book *Glory Carriers*, Jennifer Eivaz takes the reader on the journey of pursuing greater measures of God's presence. She shares her own journey openly, leaving you hungry to know Him more. With each chapter, Jennifer gently untangles common fears and misconceptions about the Holy Spirit, while at the same time encouraging you to press into more of what God has promised.

Pursuing His presence is the great call on our lives. As Christians, we have been invited into a relational journey—one between a perfect, loving God and His children. We are made in His image. He chose to create us differently from every other being in the universe. And He did so with the intent of intimacy. His focus was, and always has been, relationship. It is the foundation of every other aspect of our lives.

Jesus did not invite us to follow Him so that we could stand on a stage, declaring His existence, or so that we could see miracles. Because the Spirit of the resurrected Christ lives within us, we expect miracles. But miracles are not where

His desires are focused. He wants our hearts. He wants our absolute "yes" to a relationship with Him.

On its own, the fact that the Holy Spirit is available to us is incredible; that He endlessly pursues our hearts is breathtaking. God wants to reveal Himself to us so He can reveal Himself *through* us.

There is a profound connection between what you know about Him and what you become. Jennifer writes beautifully about this reality: "I liken this to a very real wrestling match with a good God who deeply loves you, but whose very presence demands a transformation from you." The Holy Spirit lives in every believer, and He will never leave. It is His promise. But He does not rest on everyone. Why? Not because He is overly sensitive or picky. But He is holy. Holiness is God's personal beauty. Everything we desire in life is somehow connected to holiness. Creation itself longs to see who we are. The revealing of who we are reveals who He is. It is all about Him.

To know Him clearly and reveal His nature is our greatest privilege and greatest responsibility. The Holy Spirit took up residence inside you when you became a follower of Jesus. Now, all of heaven has positioned itself to watch what you will accomplish in His name.

Bill Johnson, Bethel Church, Redding, California;
author, *Raising Giant-Killers* and *God Is Good*

Acknowledgments

This being my third book, I want to thank my amazing husband and wonderful children, who have championed and adjusted to my life as a writer. Without their support, I could not do what I do.

I also want to thank Bill Johnson and Paul Goulet, two keys in the Body of Christ, who have taught me more than most about having a real relationship with the Spirit of God.

A special thank-you to my church family, pastors and ministry leaders, who have also championed and adjusted to my writing life. Your support has not gone unnoticed.

Thank you again to Steve Shultz from the Elijah List and Elijah Streams for being the divine catalyst for God's plan in my life as a writer.

Thank you again, Virginia and Justin Meyer, for allowing me to use your spare home to work and write. You have always blessed me with a peaceful space to dwell in during times I have needed it most.

I want to especially thank my personal prayer partners who have selflessly prayed for me and for those who will read this book. Thank you, Andrea, Catherine, David, Elaina, Emmanuel, Joe, Mark, Mary, Michelle, Nathan, Sharon and Taylor.

Introduction

I was casually perusing through my digital notes on my phone and discovered a mysterious statement had been typed in. It read, "You have received the mantle of the writing sword." I am puzzled to this day as to how it got there and finally decided to just credit the Holy Spirit. Interestingly, the timing of my find occurred shortly after I had been invited by Steve Shultz to write for the Elijah List, and not too long before I was approached to write my first book with Chosen Books.

The concept of a mantle in the Bible can have various meanings, but most often it refers to a cloak, a covering, or some other type of clothing. Prophets in the Bible were apt to wear a mantle as a sign of their calling from God. We see how Elijah passed his mantle on to Elisha as a prophetic sign of his anointing and ministry coming upon his spiritual son. When Elisha picked up the mantle, he essentially picked up his calling and the miracles began to flow as well.

A mantle means heavy-duty responsibility. You lose your life, in a sense, to serving that mantle in partnership with the Holy Spirit. With that said, I do not write books for entertainment value or to advance my own personal agenda.

When I write, I create weapons to equip an army. This book that you are holding in your hand has been written to teach, train and dress you in new spiritual armaments. It will teach you about the glory of God and equip you to be a person who manifests His glory in signs and wonders. It will call you into a fierce love relationship with the Holy Spirit.

Writing this book was very different than my first two books. There is a degree of struggle to each book, but this time I felt as if I was writing straight out of a heavenly river. Words and imagery flowed with an intent to awaken and quicken you, the reader, on every page. My prayer is that the contents would call out to you even after you have put the book down and awaken your spirit to a whole new way of living.

What Is a Glory Carrier?

As a new believer, I attended my first women's retreat, led by author and intercessor Barbara Wentroble, not knowing what to expect. But once I got there, I could sense an unusual expectation and vibe coming from the other women in attendance. As we all stood in a single-file line to receive personal prayer from the minister, suddenly the air seemed to part open above us, and the raw firepower of the Holy Spirit fell upon us. The impact was obvious given the exuberant displays of emotion and unique physical responses of worship and ecstatic joy. As for me, I was deeply changed in one moment and felt a hunger for God that had far surpassed anything I had felt before.

This was my first experience with a *glory carrier*—meaning a man or woman of God who displays His manifest presence. And over the years, I have cherished sitting under the ministry of other glory carriers such as Paul Goulet, Bill Johnson and more. My thinking was, if I could attend events where such people were ministering, then I would encounter God or the miraculous in some way. After all, anyone present could receive a special anointing from the Holy Spirit they carried, right? Still, in all my experiences with these glory carriers, the idea that I, too, could become a glory carrier did not cross my mind. I loved the presence of God, but what I had seen in these leaders seemed to be hit and miss for me. When I ministered, sometimes His power was present and at other times not, and I had no idea why.

What was the secret? Where was I missing it?

I finally realized that those I have mentioned, along with many others, had all communicated a similar message about the Holy Spirit. To them the Holy Spirit was not just a power from God or a force to create a miracle service or crusade. Rather, each one communicated a deep reverence and honor for their Friend, the Holy Spirit. The result of their friendship was obvious: Supernatural signs, wonders and miracles resulted from the demonstration of God's glory.

Can you really become friends with the Spirit of God?

Every friendship has a starting point, and I believe friendship with the Holy Spirit begins with baptism in the Holy Spirit. Here is my story of meeting Him for the first time.

Befriending the Holy Spirit

At age eighteen, as a first-time visitor in a small Pentecostal church in Los Banos, California, I sat next to a petite middle-aged woman with waist-length hair, a long dress and no facial makeup. Apparently, she believed that way of dress was a requirement for holiness, and although I cannot remember exactly what I wore, I know it was not that. That was probably the second time in my life at any Christian church.

Growing up, I had been part of the Mormon Church (also known as the LDS Church) and still did not care too much for Christians.

That day I visited that peculiar little church out of sheer desperation. I knew so little about Jesus, yet suddenly He met me, and I knew without a doubt that it was Him. There was no question about it. His Presence was tangible, like a liquid warmth being poured over me. And through this one glorious encounter, everything changed. With guidance from this woman, I prayed a simple prayer for salvation and with all of my heart surrendered my life to Jesus Christ.

And then she pointed to something more, inviting me into an experience and to a lifestyle filled with the glory of the Lord. "Would you like to receive the Holy Ghost?" she asked. (The Holy Ghost is the preferred name for the Holy Spirit in her denomination.) My response was an immediate yes. Even though I did not know what to expect, I trusted what she said and received without hindrance. With one simple question, she led me into an authentic biblical experience known as the baptism of the Spirit.

When you become baptized in the Holy Spirit, you will speak in a brand-new language; only it is a heavenly language, not a natural one. Other terms for the same experience include *praying in the Spirit, speaking in an unknown tongue*, and *receiving the promise of the Father*. These terms are mentioned interchangeably throughout the New Testament and especially in Acts. Dr. Bill Hamon describes it this way:

> When we pray in tongues our praying originates and flows from our inner spirit and not from our natural mind. It is not a learned language, but a gift from the Holy Spirit. The natural mind does not understand it. "For if I pray in

19

tongues, my spirit prays, but my understanding is unfruitful"
(1 Corinthians 14:14).[1]

Within minutes of giving my life to Christ, at the encouragement of my dear sister, I began speaking in my new heavenly language. (I will explain more about baptism in the Holy Spirit in the appendix.) It was a glorious experience. Not only had I been "born of the Spirit" (John 3:8)—referring to salvation—but I had also been "clothed with power from on high" (Luke 24:49), meaning baptized in the Holy Spirit. This was my first taste of the *glory realm*, which is the realm of the Spirit, and something I will explain throughout this book.

In the days and years to follow, I found myself longing for encounters with the Spirit of God and the continuous sense of His presence. Only I did not understand Him or how to connect to Him, which left me frustrated and wanting. Perhaps you have a similar story, and this is why you are reading *Glory Carriers*, because these kinds of experiences leave a driving thirst in you.

Being Led by the Glory

Soon after my salvation and baptism in the Holy Spirit, I had a repeated thought that seemed to bubble up from the inside of me, having come directly from my spirit, not my mind. The Spirit whispered, *It's time to go to church.* I find it funny now, but would you believe that not once had I thought to do that? I only knew to go to the Mormon Church and had not yet connected that Christians go to Christian churches. I was a true "babe" in Christ and needed to be taught even the simplest things (see Hebrews 5:13).

My mother and stepfather, also new believers in Christ, were attending a large and popular Baptist church in Modesto,

California. I decided, especially after hearing this instruction from the Spirit, to attend with them. I joined their college group, including the new believers class, and began memorizing foundational Bible verses that grounded me in my new faith. With the help of this church, I became rooted in my core Christian beliefs while making several new friends my age, allowing me to let go of my old ones.

As much as I enjoyed what I was learning and the synergy of my new friendships, there was a gnawing discontent inside of me. I felt as if I was missing something. I was looking for and longing for the perceptible presence of God. This church had great impact on my foundation and taught me to hide the word in my heart, but I cannot recall a single discussion, teaching or recognizable moment with the Holy Spirit.

After about four months, I made a sudden decision, to the angst of my family, to begin attending a small Foursquare church. My family tried to reason with me that we should all be in church together. I understood their logic, but my hunger for the Spirit was driving my decision. That Foursquare church provided another valuable season of growth, but I soon made one more move to a very large Pentecostal church in the same city. This church was my favorite. Not only was there a large group of people my age, but they also had a Bible school. Most importantly, however, in this fellowship the people were often healed and delivered miraculously, and they practiced the gifts of speaking in tongues and interpretation, spontaneous prophetic songs and dance and much more. I had found the environment I was looking for.

Feeling God's Manifest Glory

Apostle Guillermo Maldonado, senior leader of King Jesus International Ministry, describes the presence of God as being an environment. He explains in his book *The Glory of God* how God created the oceans and rivers as a sustainable, life-giving environment for fish and other creatures. Just the same, He created Eden as the perfect environment for human beings. "God put Adam right into the environment of His presence and glory. . . . That was the only environment in which he could be sustained and thrive."[2]

When Adam and Eve went against God's command to not eat from the Tree of Knowledge of Good and Evil, they had to be removed from the environment of Eden to safeguard them from eating from the other tree, the Tree of Life, and living forever in their fallen state (see Genesis 3:22–23). Now severed from the life-flow of God, Adam and Eve began to experience all the effects of death, as they were no longer in the environment that sustained them. They were no longer living in the habitation of His glorious presence.[3]

One of the attributes of God is that He is omnipresent. The prefix used here, *omni-*, is a Latin word that means "all."[4] God is all-present, meaning He is everywhere all at the same time. He is not confined to time or space, and no one can hide from Him or escape His notice. King David spoke into this when he wrote, "Where can I go from your Spirit? Where can I flee from your presence?" (Psalm 139:7). The prophet Jeremiah was also inspired to write, "'Am I only a God nearby,' declares the LORD, 'and not a God far away? Who can hide in secret places so that I cannot see them?' . . . 'Do not I fill heaven and earth?'" (Jeremiah 23:23–24). We have all heard of people who were described as "far from God" or "running from God."

Chase Yettman, facilities director for Harvest Christian Center in Turlock, California, describes his youth as being full of rebellion even though his mother was a very strong Christian. He intentionally avoided anything that had to do with God to the point of drugs, theft and even homelessness. "I had a very adverse reaction to God and His Church," he said. "Looking back, I know for certain that He protected me despite my attitude and saved my life many times over." Some do run and hide from God, but none can achieve any real distance from Him. His very nature is omnipresent, which means that everywhere you go He is already there.

Even though God is omnipresent, this reality is not always discernable through our senses, which explains the apostle Paul's encouragement that we ought to "live by faith, not by sight" (2 Corinthians 5:7). From ancient times, people identified that God actively watched over them and protected them wherever they went. In Genesis 16:13, for example, Hagar referred to the Lord as "the God who sees." Later, the prophet Isaiah conveyed the heart of the Lord saying, "When you pass through the waters, I will be with you; and when you pass through the rivers, they will not sweep over you. When you walk through the fire, you will not be burned; the flames will not set you ablaze" (Isaiah 43:2).

These passages can provide temporary comfort to our soul, but many people struggle to reconcile these truths emotionally. What they read about and what they feel and experience on most days are two different things. And when we cannot discern His presence in a continuous and identifiable way, it can lead us into feeling distant with God. Our perception, then, is that He must not be close. This is not truth, but more of a perceived reality based on our experience. This is true even in our natural relationships.

For example, if I did not have regular contact and communication with my husband, Ron, I would feel quite disconnected over time. Ron and I know that we need more than text messages and email to create a highly connected relationship. We have to be in each other's presence and have lengthy dialogues face-to-face in order to feel bonded.

In the same way, many struggle to feel attached to the Person of the Holy Spirit based on what they only read about Him. Just as we have to experience people in order to know them and feel connected, in the same manner we have to experience the Person of the Holy Spirit. Another name for Him in the Bible is the "Spirit of glory" (1 Peter 4:14), which obviously implies the supernatural and the miraculous. When we experience Him, we will experience His glory because that is who He is.

Getting Hungry for His Presence

Just as infants cry out for food and comfort, as new believers our spirits cry out for the only one who can satisfy, the Holy Spirit. I was steadily growing in my faith and developing a track record for answered prayer. From time to time I would encounter the Holy Spirit by experiencing an aspect of His miraculous nature, but almost always in the setting of a powerful church service. In other words, I would be at church in the right place at the right time where His glory just happened to be manifesting. Such encounters would always reflect His nature, namely that He is personal and He is supernatural. These were the "moments" and "windows in time" that sustained and encouraged me, only I was not satisfied. What I was really after was the continuous feeling of His presence in my life—whether I was in church or not. I felt strongly that I should have the distinct awareness of His presence continuously. Even though I prayed often, worshiped and meditated in His Word, I could not feel Him at all. My perceived reality, as I explained earlier, was that He must not be near but far away.

During my second year of college in Modesto, California, I participated in the InterVarsity ministry and was asked to be in a leadership role and teach a Bible study. The only problem was that I did not have much knowledge of the Bible; I had only been saved for a year. But there was another young man on the team who committed to teaching a campus Bible study. He was really smart, and I would attend his group, take notes and then teach his notes to my group. His name was Ron Eivaz—and we have partnered in the Word and in ministry ever since.

Halfway through our education, Ron and I left California to finish our degrees at Oral Roberts University in Tulsa, Oklahoma. We did not know of any university at the time that allowed us to earn our college degrees while being immersed in a Holy Spirit filled and globally minded environment. Despite ministry involvement, I still struggled to find the presence of God on a personal level.

In my final year at Oral Roberts University, I distinctly remember crying out to God with tears and deep frustration in my dorm room, "Where are you? Are you even here? I can't *feel* you!" Keep in mind, I had already lived through extraordinary spiritual warfare and I was no stranger to the supernatural and how that impacted my senses. But it was no substitute for an encounter with the Holy Spirit.

Suddenly I heard an audible voice in the room. I believe it was the voice of the Spirit, and He said, *I am closer than you think!*

His response silenced my cry but did not satisfy the ache that I felt.

King David revealed an emotion that helped me to process this. He wrote, "My soul longs, yes, even faints, for the courts of the LORD; my heart and my flesh cry out for the living God" (Psalm 84:2 NKJV). I was crying out to know His presence beyond just an intellectual knowledge. I wanted to sense and experience His presence continuously.

Was this just a maturity issue? Definitely, as I was still growing in my awareness of His presence. Still, the Bible describes, "For as many as are led by the Spirit of God, these are sons of God" (Romans 8:14 NKJV). How can you be led by the Spirit of God before sensing His presence? Far too many people believe it is normal to not have any awareness of Him at all. Is this you? Have you, too, had a life-changing encounter with the Holy Spirit, only now you cannot feel His presence continually?

You see, too many people misunderstand who the Holy Spirit is largely due to a lack of teaching. Many think of Him as a force or an "It." Or they pursue just the benefits of the Holy Spirit, such as supernatural power and anointing, without pursuing a relationship with the Person of the Holy Spirit. He is a Person. He is God. He has personality, intelligence, will and feelings. When we honor Him and lovingly acknowledge Him, He will respond with His Presence.

Paul Goulet, senior leader of the International Church of Las Vegas, described to me repeatedly how He invites the Holy Spirit's deep friendship and leading daily. "Holy Spirit, come and possess me!" he would say. I could tell by the miracles that flowed through his life, whom he had spent time with, that he had been with the Spirit of God. And after hearing that I, too, could have a friendship with the Holy Spirit, from Paul and others, I began a personal journey to find out how.

Here is what I discovered. In the context of prayer, I began talking to the Holy Spirit, inviting His presence and requesting His friendship. I have heard some people express a concern that they are offending Jesus by doing this. I want to assure you that Jesus is not offended by your communication with the Spirit of God. God the Father, Son and Holy Spirit are not in competition with one another. They are perfectly unified.

I continued to invite the Holy Spirit to make Himself known in my life, even asking Him to teach me how to be His friend. Nothing seemed to change for a long time, but then one day I noticed something new. Upon my invitation, I discerned His presence enter the room I was in and then come upon my person. This began to happen on a regular basis. When I say that I could discern His presence "come upon my person," what I am trying to describe is the constant touch of a Friend. For example, I can feel His hands on the back of my shoulders in a very comforting way at times, or I sense His joyful face in front of my face and looking at me. At times He stands peacefully beside me; at other times He wraps me in a supernaturally charged blanket, which is how I would describe the embrace of the Holy Spirit.

Finally, I had crossed a barrier after years of pursuing the Holy Spirit. I could now feel His presence as being with me, and I felt this with regularity. The only drawback was the painful awareness of when His manifest presence was not there. To be honest, the absence of His felt presence shaped holiness into my life more than anything else. Please do not misunderstand this. I was not this horrible person with a double standard or a double life. Nevertheless, He is *holy*, and my bad attitudes grieved Him, disrupting our connection. I committed to change no matter what it took. I had to have His presence with me at all times.

Has my life changed because of my growing friendship with the Holy Spirit? Absolutely. I have seen more of His manifest glory than ever before. I have witnessed more miracles, more deliverances and more lives dramatically changed. Yet I am keenly aware that there is so much more. It is not easy to carry the glory of God within the delicate container of friendship with the Holy Spirit—a costly yet priceless relationship.

Learning to Identify the Spirit Personally

Karen first encountered the Holy Spirit on her birthday in upstate New York. At her birthday gathering, she decided to give her life to Christ at the urging of her daughter. Her daughter also led her into receiving the baptism of the Holy Spirit. Karen began speaking in tongues and described her behavior as somewhat hysterical because she had no idea what tongues were. Thankfully, Karen then felt the glory of God descend upon her as a peaceful but tingly sensation. This experience later helped her to identify the Holy Spirit in church services and in prayer groups that she attended. Eventually she could identify His presence in her own prayer times in the same manner, something that brought her much comfort.

Knowing that God is omnipresent is a powerful thought, but not one we can always relate to in day-to-day life. Knowledge alone does not satisfy our deeper desire for connection with God. We need to also encounter God's manifest presence, which is synonymous with encountering His glory. When He manifests His glory, much like Karen discovered, we will experience something supernatural and identifiable. And just for clarification, the Holy Spirit is often called the third Person of the Godhead: namely, God the Father, God the Son and God the Holy Spirit. Being spoken of as third, however, is not a ranking or an indicator of being less than. The Holy Spirit is an equal. Father, Son and Spirit—they are all God, one divine being expressed as three different personalities.

A triune understanding of God gives context for Bible passages such as Genesis 1:26, which reads, "Then God said,

'Let us make mankind in our image,'" and Isaiah 6:8: "Then I heard the voice of the Lord saying, 'Whom shall I send? And who will go for us?'" Here we glimpse into the mystery of the Trinity. He is One God in three Persons, and their unity is evident. In the Old Testament, His glory was also seen by Moses at the burning bush, the wandering Israelites as a fire by night and a cloud by day, and then by the priests as a cloud of glory that filled the temple, causing them to fall on their faces before Him (see Exodus 3:2; 13:21–22; 2 Chronicles 5:13–14).

Jesus said, "I and My Father are One" (John 10:30 NKJV), and before He left the earth, He promised to send us the Holy Spirit. "And I will ask the Father, and he will give you another advocate to help you and be with you forever—the Spirit of truth" (14:16–17). The Holy Spirit is ever-present for believers because He dwells in us. This is in stark contrast with the Old Testament, when the Holy Spirit would come or go depending on what level of anointing was needed to serve God's purposes.

For believers, however, He dwells within us always once we make Jesus lord over our lives. This is defined as the indwelling of the Spirit. He dwells within us and turns our physical bodies into a home. Paul makes this point in 1 Corinthians 6:19: "Do you not know that your bodies are temples of the Holy Spirit?" Elsewhere in the New Testament, we see His glory manifested through the Person of the Holy Spirit, who is also called the "Spirit of Christ" (Romans 8:9; 1 Peter 1:11; Galatians 4:6).

The indwelling of the Spirit, however, is not the same as the manifest presence of the Spirit. When the Holy Spirit manifests in glory, again, by definition, you will experience—perhaps even see—something. The Spirit of glory fell like fire upon the disciples in the Upper Room, when He shook the building in response to their prayers for more boldness, and when He knocked Saul to the ground to prepare him to be converted to Christ and accept his heavenly calling (see Acts 2:3; 4:31; 9:3).

Pressing Deeper into His Glory

The apostle Peter had a deep and intimate relationship with the Holy Spirit. We know this by reading the evidence alone that he was a glory carrier. When Peter walked down the street, people were healed in the presence of his shadow (see Acts 5:15).

Remember how I described the embrace of the Holy Spirit as like being wrapped in a supernaturally charged blanket? I believe Peter lived in the embrace of the Spirit of God. He had become overshadowed by the glory in the Person of the Holy Spirit, and what overshadowed him then overshadowed the people he came into contact with. The results were miraculous.

Like Peter and other heroes of faith, you are being summoned to be a glory carrier. Do not mistake this call as a call for somebody else. This is for you. The Holy Spirit is no respecter of persons. He does not play favorites, but honors all who honor Him.

Are you ready to begin your journey into the glory? If so, then let's begin by first reaching out to the Spirit of God in prayer.

Say this prayer with me:

Holy Spirit, I come to you in the name of Jesus. I honor and worship You as the Spirit of Christ and acknowledge and honor Your Lordship over my life. I invite You to possess every part of me and to teach me how to walk in friendship with You. Come and meet with me here and share Your heart with me. I am listening.

Now just be still and wait. Do not rush. Listen for His still small voice. His voice will come to you as words, as flowing thoughts or as pictures. Write down what comes to you and ask Him for more clarity on whatever you believe He shows you. Write it down and treat it like precious treasure.

Prayer is the first step into a deep relationship and friendship with the Spirit of God. Prayer is daily and continuous. In prayer we will hear His desires and in turn we can share ours. Let's begin to press in deeper. Let's ask the Holy Spirit to show us His glory.

KINGDOM PRINCIPLES

1. A glory carrier is one who visibly and consistently demonstrates the glory of God through supernatural signs and wonders—the fruit of discovering deep reverence for and friendship with the Spirit of God.

2. Every friendship has a starting point. I believe friendship with the Holy Spirit begins with baptism in the Holy Spirit. Through this experience you will receive a heavenly language and power from on high (see Luke 24:49).

3. Many struggle to feel attached to the Person of the Holy Spirit based on what they only read about Him. Just as we have to experience people in order to know them and feel connected, in the same manner we have to experience the Person of the Holy Spirit.

4. Another name for the Holy Spirit in the Bible is the "Spirit of glory" (1 Peter 4:14), which obviously implies

the supernatural and the miraculous. When we experience Him, we will experience His glory, because that is who He is.

5. The indwelling of the Spirit is not the same as the manifest presence of the Spirit. When the Holy Spirit manifests in glory, you will feel, and perhaps even see, something tangible.

THOUGHTS FOR REFLECTION

1. Far too many people believe it is normal to not sense the presence of the Holy Spirit. Have you, however, had a life-changing encounter with Him? If so, has this encounter left you wanting more?

2. How can you be led by the Spirit of God before sensing His presence? Do you know what His presence feels like? If so, how would you describe it?

3. Have you ever considered talking directly to the Spirit of God? If so, what would you like to say to Him?

4. What are your thoughts on having an actual friendship with the Holy Spirit? Does that challenge you, excite you, or both?

5. Are you ready to begin your journey into the glory? If so, what is your next step?

Show Me Your Glory

If we define the glory of God as the manifest presence of God, then a glory carrier is one who displays the glory of God in a visible way that is both miraculous and reflects God's character. The demonstration of glory can never be produced through some kind of religious methodology or spiritual formula; rather, it flows supernaturally from our intimate friendship with the manifest presence of God, the Holy Spirit.

One way that God reveals His glory is in the form of light, an act that powerfully declares His nature: "God is light; in him there is no darkness at all" (1 John 1:5). The word *light* in this passage can also mean "radiance."[1]

On occasion the glory of God has come upon my life just like that, as a radiance. The first time I know of happened at a local restaurant. The manager commented to my husband and me that we had an "aura" of light around us. I realize the term *aura* can be a New Age term to describe a supernatural emanation, but she was not a believer in Jesus. She was using the only language that she knew to describe God's light radiating off us, something He allowed her to see.

At a recent conference, two pastors shared a similar testimony with me. They both said that before I made an altar call, my eyes became transparent, as if with purity and holiness, then began to glow. They observed this a few moments before God's power fell upon those waiting to be prayed for. There are also two documented times that my entire being has glowed in God's outstandingly bright light from head to toe. I have photos of these incidents. All of these experiences were deeply humbling, as such a display of glory can cause you to feel undeserving.

You Get Your Clothes Back

Some have suggested that Adam and Eve were clothed in God's glorious light rather than in natural clothing.[2] "Yet you made them only a little lower than God and crowned them with glory and honor" (Psalm 8:5 NLT). The Hebrew word for "crowned" in this passage can mean "to surround" and "to encircle (for . . . protection)."[3] I believe this could mean that Adam and Eve were covered and clothed with God's glory being they were encircled in His brilliant light.

After Adam and Eve violated God's command to "not eat from the tree of the knowledge of good and evil, for when you eat from it you will certainly die" (Genesis 2:17), their lives changed dramatically.

One of the things we can surmise is that through their sin they lost their brilliant covering of light as the kingdom of darkness came in and afflicted their entire world. Glory-carrying humanity who would rejoice at the approaching sound of God's presence now hid from Him in terror for the first time.

But the LORD God called to the man, "Where are you?" He answered, "I heard you in the garden, and I was afraid because I was naked; so I hid." And he said, "Who told you that you were naked? Have you eaten from the tree that I commanded you not to eat from?"

3:9–11

In His fatherly goodness, instead of leaving them to fend for themselves, God made new coverings for Adam and Eve by killing an animal, shedding its blood in the process, and then clothing them with the skins. This is such a touching prophetic picture. He was pointing to the day of passionate restoration when the shed blood of Jesus would fully cover our sins and the Holy Spirit would clothe us in His beautiful glory once again.

As powerful as this picture is, being repositioned as a glory carrier requires a kind of heart intimacy that forsakes all superficiality with God. "And we all, with unveiled face, continually seeing as in a mirror the glory of the Lord, are progressively being transformed into His image from [one degree of] glory to [even more] glory, which comes from the Lord, [who is] the Spirit" (2 Corinthians 3:18 AMP).

Having an "unveiled face" means that we no longer hide our hearts in fear of being seen and known by God. We become wholehearted in our devotion and "free from all reserve or hesitation."[4] If anything stands in the way of wholehearted devotion toward God, a glory carrier will do whatever it takes to remove any hindrances within the relationship. This includes dealing with any deep, irrational fears we might have of the Holy Spirit.

Have you ever been afraid of someone and unable to have an authentic relationship with that person? We have all experienced this from time to time with people, but what do you do if you are afraid of the Holy Spirit?

I was hindered at times in my relationship with the Spirit because I feared Him in an unhealthy way. I had read the stern warning of Jesus as to how we should treat the Holy Spirit. He said, "Truly I tell you, people can be forgiven all their sins and every slander they utter, but whoever blasphemes against the Holy Spirit will never be forgiven; they are guilty of an eternal sin" (Mark 3:28–29).

I had also read about Ananias and Sapphira, a husband and wife who attempted to be deceptive in their giving. Peter discerned their sin by the Holy Spirit and rebuked Ananias, saying, "You haven't lied to men, but to God." Immediately he died. Later his wife, Sapphira, came in and she, too, lied about their offering. She claimed it was the full amount from a sale of property when it was not, something she could have said truthfully without any repercussions. She also died instantly, having come under the judgment of the Lord.

When I first read that passage in Acts 5 as an immature believer, I concluded, based on my emotions, that the Holy Spirit was too scary, much more so than Jesus or our heavenly Father. I thought, *It's better, then, to keep Him at a distance . . . just in case.*

Now hopefully neither you nor I would ever lie to the Holy Spirit or blaspheme the Holy Spirit, but we may have felt an irrational fear in connection to the Holy Spirit. Have you distanced yourself because you are worried that you might have offended Him or blasphemed Him? If so, I want to assure you that your concern demonstrates His conviction still active in your heart, which is a sure sign that He is with you and has not left you. If that is you, I am inviting you back into relationship with Him, because a glory carrier can have no such distance with the Spirit of glory. They must risk it all and fully entrust their life to Him.

Still, I have learned how genuine authenticity with a powerful Friend can be daunting, even terrifying, at times. Australian minister and author Phil Mason wrote how Jesus "refused to do superficiality. This is why the disciples were tempted to turn back on so many occasions."[5] The reward of the unveiled heart, however, is an encounter with His glorious light, which drives deep darkness and bondage away from you. Little by little, you transform back into His glorious likeness in every way. You get your clothes back, and they are clothes of glory.

You Become a Deliverer

People who deliver others from demonic bondage are those who have first been delivered themselves. Take, for example, Michelle Passey from Washington State, who was saved and delivered from demonic bondage in a prophetic dream and has ministered powerfully in the prophetic and in deliverance ever since. Sharing her unusual testimony with me, she said:

> It was March 2003 and I had just given birth to my fourth child. He was only a few weeks old and my marriage was in big trouble. I was a broken shell of a woman and not in a healthy state of mind. If it weren't for my newborn, I would have tried to kill myself.
>
> I had been brought up knowing about Jesus and even as a child I had given my life to Him. As a teen and into my thirties, my life didn't belong to Him at all. I was totally living for myself. I had a dream, however, that changed everything. I had gone to bed knowing I needed to change, but not knowing how. And I was desperate.
>
> I dreamt I was standing with Jesus looking at complete darkness. I could hear all kinds of screaming and could feel an intense fear. I took His hand and said, "What you are

showing me is frightening me!" The scene changed and now I am standing on a stage/platform, and I'm preaching to a crowd of people.

The Lord was showing me my choices. I had two paths, and only I could choose which one I was going to take. He was showing me my call as a pastor. He was giving me my hope back.

In the dream, I wholeheartedly chose Him! When I woke up, I noticed a freedom I had never known before. My mind was clear from all the noise. I no longer wanted to die and was excited to live. I was delivered from all kinds of unclean spirits, and I no longer wanted to do things I previously couldn't stop doing. My heart fully belonged to Jesus, and I've been ignited for Him ever since without stopping.

We also see this displayed in the life of Moses, a man used powerfully by God to deliver the nation of Israel from bitter, hard bondage to Egypt. I believe the seeds for deliverance were deposited into Moses as a newborn baby. Moses was birthed under the harshest of edicts from Egypt's king, the pharaoh, who feared a potential uprising from the growing Hebrew population. Pharaoh's solution, then, was to murder all the baby Hebrew boys by drowning them in the Nile River.

Interestingly, the king perceived no threat from females, yet it was a few fearless females who banded together to preserve Moses' life. Unable to keep her baby hidden and safe, his mother, Jochebed, concealed him in a basket on the side of the river while his sister Miriam kept an eye on him from a distance. When Pharaoh's daughter went to the Nile to bathe, she felt sorry for the crying infant and drew him out of the river of death, thus the name Moses, meaning "drawn . . . out (of the water)."[6] Then, in a disguised act of divine retribution, she brought the future upriser into her father's palace as her own son. In addition, and at the advice of young Miriam, she allowed Moses to be nursed by his biological mother until he was weaned. How fitting that his mother's name means "Jehovah is glory,"[7] seeing that Moses was preserved by the Lord of glory so he could eventually carry His glory.

As Moses grew into adulthood, his divine call to deliver his nation began to outweigh his need to keep a privileged and protected Egyptian life. Moses deeply empathized with the injustice against his people—so much so that he murdered one of his fellow Egyptians for beating a Hebrew slave. This act incited Pharaoh to try to assassinate him, but Moses fled from the enraged king to go live in Midian. Here again, he collides with injustice, but this time with a much better outcome. When a band of abusive shepherds chased off seven sisters from a watering well, Moses immediately raised a defense. Like a true deliverer, he not only contended with the abusers but also cared for the sisters by filling their watering troughs. Their father, a Midianite priest named Reuel, who also went by the name Jethro, repaid Moses' bravery by inviting him to a family meal and later giving him a daughter as a wife. The name Reuel means "a friend of God"[8] (or we could just as easily say "an intimate of God"). I believe Reuel, by his very name, was a prophetic overture to Moses as to what kind of relationship Moses would ultimately have with the Lord of glory.

Over time, Moses developed a very intimate friendship with God. We see their portraiture of intimacy as being two dear friends who spoke face-to-face with one another (see Exodus 33:11). Their relationship did not begin that way, however. When God's manifest presence was first revealed to Moses, He was revealed in the flames of fire within a bush, only the bush did not burn up. While leading the desert flocks, this phenomenal sight in nature caught Moses' attention. He drew near the burning bush in curiosity, but once

God saw him, He spoke out, "Do not come any closer. . . . Take off your sandals, for the place where you are standing is holy ground" (3:5). His reverberant words and presence utterly overwhelmed Moses, so much so that Moses hid his face from Him in fear (see v. 6).

You Turn Your Face toward God

I was pleasantly surprised to discover the meaning of the word *worship* in the New Testament. It means "to kiss."[9] Although the meaning is largely metaphorical, it portrays our relationship with the Holy Spirit as being face-to-face with nothing hidden. Our tendency, however, is to do the opposite.

Have you ever tried to hide from the manifest presence of God? I sure have. Although He does not seek to embarrass or shame His children, His glory will reveal to you any darkness still resident in your soul. This is something you have to settle within yourself. If you are going to be a glory carrier, you must lay your heart bare in the presence of the Lord and trust Him with the outcome.

Several years ago, I went to a large conference at the International Church of Las Vegas to hear an unusual speaker. They said he was uncommonly gifted in giving words of knowledge, which is the supernatural ability to know a fact about a person, present or past, that you could not possibly know unless the Holy Spirit revealed it to you. We read about it in 1 Corinthians 12:8. This speaker, for example, would know by the revelation of the Spirit your name, where you worked, what city you were from and much more, and I was interested in seeing a deeper expression of this gift.

What I did not expect was a man who also carried the glory of God in a way I could feel. I was not prepared to feel

His presence on this level and found myself watching him minister powerfully to others in the room while I hid as best I could behind the seats so as to not be seen or ministered to. I realized years later that I had chosen to veil myself in the presence of God's glory and essentially hid from my Healer and restrained my Deliverer.

Can I encourage you to not do what I did? I wonder to this day what life-changing ministry that I missed receiving from the presence of His glory because I was too afraid. There is a real temptation to hide our face from the presence of a relationship-seeking God because of His glory and power test us. Still, He sees you and me with a much different lens than we see ourselves, only He does not change who He is to make us more comfortable.

You Seek His Glory

In Exodus 19, the Lord shared with Moses His tremendous heart and vision for His people, the Israelites. Consider that God had spared nothing and no one to set His people free from the Egyptians. He had engaged a masterful display of deliverance, beginning with the ten plagues and finishing with the miraculous parting of the Red Sea. God fought hard for Israel because He loved her and was preparing the entire nation to carry His glory. He said to Moses,

> "You yourselves have seen what I did to Egypt, and how I carried you on eagles' wings and brought you to myself. Now if you obey me fully and keep my covenant, then out of all nations you will be my treasured possession. Although the whole earth is mine, you will be for me a kingdom of priests and a holy nation."

vv. 4–6

I am amazed that God could look at a nation populated by broken, testy slaves and foresee their transformation into royal and holy ministers of His presence. God's magnificent words through Moses touched their hearts and they responded, "We will do everything the LORD has said" (v. 8). I believe they were sincere, though they could not embrace the challenge of closeness with an all-powerful God.

The Lord then called the entire nation to assemble at the low point of Mount Sinai so He could speak directly to all of them. He descended upon this great mountain in the form of illuminating fire, along with thick smoke, roaring thunder and streaks of lightning. His intensity and glory evoked a deep fear in the Israelites, however.

They were so frightened by the Lord's appearance that they distanced themselves from the mountain, saying to Moses, "Speak to us yourself and we will listen. But do not have God speak to us or we will die" (20:19). Moses passionately urged them to stay put "so that the fear of God will be with you to keep you from sinning" (v. 20). The Israelites remained distant but said repeatedly they would obey the Lord.

If only they would have joined their words with nearness to the glory! The fear of the Lord, then, would have been sealed into their hearts. Without it, they engaged all too easily in idolatry and its abominable practices, which cost them the glory and protection of God.

Monica (not her real name) often wrestled in her relationship with God and in her relationship with others. When she felt safe and secure, she was very worshipful, prayerful and authentically prophetic. When she did not feel safe and secure, she would become sporadic in her church attendance and resisted the loving communication that came from her church family. Proximity with the presence of God brought her noticeable transformation. But when she withdrew, she would turn back to the familiar idols of alcohol and other vices to fill the void that only Jesus could fill. This, unfortunately, gave access to demons to bind her spiritually, and when she could not stand it anymore, she would come back to her church family, almost always needing deliverance from demons.

Her story is so common. Like the Israelites, proximity to the presence brings the fear of the Lord and transformation. Distance brings destruction.

You Become Desperate for Change

The seventy elders, the priests and Moses ate a covenant meal while the Lord stood nearby. He then summoned Moses to join Him on the mountain and said, "I will give you the tablets of stone with the law and commandments I have written for their instruction" (Exodus 24:12). What a profound honor Moses received from the Lord that day in front of all the Israelites. You would have thought, after all the signs, wonders and miracles the Lord had performed, that the Israelites would have feared Him and respected the leadership of Moses. Sadly, that did not happen.

As Moses spent forty days and nights on the mountain in the presence of the Lord, a horrible digression occurred among the Israelites. They demanded that Aaron, Moses' brother and their priest, make them an idol to worship in the place of God. Aaron complied all too easily, and they traded God's glory for a graven image of a golden calf. When Moses left the mountain and found his people celebrating the calf just like their former Egyptian taskmasters, he went into a passionate outrage. He broke the stone tablets into pieces, burned the golden calf and ground it to powder, then poured it out on the water and forced the people to drink it. Then he ordered the faithful Levites to begin killing those calf worshipers with the sword, killing about three thousand, before the Lord Himself sent a plague against the people as well.

We must learn from their mistakes. Resisting His glory, turning our faces and hiding our hearts, will remove us from the supernatural encounters we absolutely need to transform us. The Israelites' initial choice to distance themselves from the challenging presence of God became their destruction later. It also put their leader into a personal crisis, especially when God threatened to revoke His presence permanently in response to their idolatry. I believe all this pushed Moses into a desperate prayer before the Lord. As he engaged the mercy of God to preserve a future for the Israelites, he also made a bold request: "Now show me your glory" (33:18). Moses needed something to change . . . or else. He needed the kind of change that only comes from an encounter with glory.

God responded favorably to his request, but ever so carefully, because the revealed goodness of His glory could have slayed Moses. It was just too powerful. And so God put His protective hand over Moses and then hid him in the cleft of the rock as He allowed His glory to pass by him (see 33:21; 34:5–6). This beautiful encounter was enough to transform Moses into a glory carrier quite unlike before. In subsequent meetings, his very face and countenance began to radiate with the light of God, so much so that it frightened Aaron and the other Israelites. Moses remedied their fright by covering his face with a veil when he was with the people. When he went before God, however, he took the veil off. He never hid his face from God.

44

You Go from Glory to Glory

Glory carriers seem to be constantly changing, molding and moving with the impulses of the Holy Spirit. Guillermo Maldonado said, "When we are in the presence of the Lord, we go 'from glory to glory' (2 Corinthians 3:18). No one goes from one place to another without moving. God is active and moving constantly, and He manifests Himself where He desires. And when we are in Him, we move with Him."[10] As you press in for wholehearted relationship with the Spirit of glory, there will be unavoidable collisions with transformation along your journey. Ultimately it is beautiful and miraculous, but such seasons can feel like an absolute undoing as transformation happens on His terms and not ours.

Moses was a powerful forerunner of this. He demonstrated relationship with a glorious Father, but an astonishingly difficult relationship as they contended and wrestled with each other over the fate of the nation. Still, this manifested in the visible glory of God upon his countenance even though it came with a personal cost. Moses did not have a theology or a method to radiate the glory of the Lord. He just kept going back to God, again and again, in authentic friendship, and we see the results.

I have found that authenticity with God is much easier said than done, but it is so worth it. There is a reward to transformation, but it requires diligence to keep presenting our hearts openly and honestly and allowing our Friend, the Holy Spirit, to access our deep thoughts, whims and desires. This is not a one-sided relationship, however. He has a much deeper desire toward us—to come abide with us continuously rather than visit us occasionally.

Evangelist and author Michael Lombardo shared his powerful transformation from hedonism to Jesus after an encounter with the glory of God in his book *Immersed in His Glory*. Hedonism is defined as the pursuit of pleasure and sensual indulgence. Michael wrote, "Growing up, I was a partier, drug abuser, womanizer, and rebel. My teenage years were spent chasing carnal pleasure. If it made me high, I wanted to try it."[11] Michael was spiraling out of control, unable to control his passions and addictions, but the prayers of his family began to break through the barriers in his soul. He said, "I'd sit in my room, open my Bible, and the Scriptures began to intrigue me like never before." Satan fought back, however, and began to attack him fiercely as he was searching for God and for answers. Terrible thoughts of suicide began to consume his mind. He became so desperate in his struggle with suicide that with his heart laid bare before Jesus, tears running down his face, he cried out to God for a change. "Suddenly, like a mighty rushing wind, I felt the power and glory of His presence all around me. Instantly, my heart was consumed with His love and chills ran down my spine from His touch."[12] Michael was transformed that day in the glory because an encounter with glory will change you. He is now a full-time evangelist with a global signs and wonders ministry.

Are you desperate for change? Have you come to the end of yourself? Personal transformation always transpires in the presence of the glory of the Lord. His penetrating light comes upon you and begins to work its way through you. Keep going after His glory. Keep pressing into a deep friendship with the Holy Spirit. In time, others will know you have been in His presence when they see His light on you.

The Holy Spirit's expressions of glory are multidimensional and multifaceted. Glory carriers, over time, begin to recognize the various manifestations of His presence, understanding the significance and unique message behind each one of them.

One aspect of His presence, the Shekinah glory, can be seen in miraculous form, but behind it is the notion that He has come to dwell with us. This is the subject of my next chapter.

KINGDOM PRINCIPLES

1. The demonstration of glory can never be produced through some kind of religious methodology or spiritual formula; rather, it flows supernaturally from our intimate friendship with the manifest presence of God, the Holy Spirit.

2. One way that God reveals His glory is in the form of light, an act that powerfully declares His nature: "God is light, in him is no darkness at all" (1 John 1:5 KJV). Just like Moses, people have radiated the visible light of God on their faces or physical form.

3. Adam and Eve were covered and clothed with God's glory but lost their covering of light when they sinned against God. Demonic darkness entered their entire world, causing them to hide from God in shame and fear. We have hidden from God ever since.

4. Personal transformation always transpires in the presence of God's glory—only we cannot hide from it because we are afraid or ashamed. We need encounters with His glory if we are going to change. His glory challenges any darkness still resident in our souls. It drives deep darkness and bondage away from us.

5. To be a glory carrier requires a kind of heart intimacy that forsakes all superficiality with God. Having an unveiled face means that I am vulnerable, authentic and mask-less before Him. The reward of the unveiled heart

is that it can successfully encounter His glorious light and eventually reflect it in a way that can be seen.

THOUGHTS FOR REFLECTION

1. To be a glory carrier requires our wholehearted devotion to the Holy Spirit. Is there anything hindering wholeheartedness in your relationship with Him? Are you willing to do whatever it takes to remove it?

2. Do you have an unhealthy fear of the Holy Spirit? If so, are you ready to give your fear to Him so as to close the distance between you? He is inviting you into a new level of trust and to risk it all in relationship with Him.

3. There is a real temptation to hide one's face from the presence of a relationship-seeking God. How are you embracing the challenge of closeness with an all-powerful Friend?

4. When His glory manifests in power, are you able to remain in the atmosphere of glory even when you feel uncomfortable? Why or why not?

5. As you encounter the glory of the Lord, do you find yourself wanting more and more?

The Shekinah Glory

Around 2003, Ron and I attended an evening session at a conference in Fremont, California, along with other spiritually hungry people who wanted to learn about supernatural ministry and receive prayer from a man named Randy Clark. Having heard testimonies of outstanding healing miracles taking place, we had begun following Randy's powerful and compelling ministry. His candid, disarming and down-to-earth style, combined with simple and relatable teaching, made him a great example of a glory carrier. After listening to his audios, we desired a greater anointing (power from the Holy Spirit to accomplish a specific task or purpose) for more effectual and supernatural ministry.

So Ron and I went to Randy's conference and, despite our exhaustion from a jam-packed workday, waited in line for over two hours to receive a few moments of personal prayer at the end of the session. Finally, Randy approached us, laid his hands on us, and prayed for us to receive from the Holy Spirit. (The laying on of hands is a biblical act in which "one person places his hands upon the body of another person, with some definite spiritual purpose."[1]) I was sure we would feel the power of the Holy Spirit or have a tangible experience as hands were laid on us, something to prove we had received, but neither of us felt a thing.

With disappointment, I thought, *Did we waste our time and energy? Did we come here for nothing?* Almost as soon as I thought it, Randy said, "Just like I did not feel anything during a time when hands were laid on me and I received, I pray that You, Holy Spirit, would do the same for them and let them go home and see the results." Randy, here, spoke prophetically that God's presence would go with us and be seen, that we would experience the visible manifestation of His glory.

In that season of pastoring, Ron and I both led midweek gatherings at our church in addition to our regular Sunday services. At Ron's midweek service, he taught the men in attendance about the remarkable anointing of the Holy Spirit for supernatural healing. As he did, the Spirit of glory descended upon the men like a refreshing rain. I cannot say this is typical, but here it resulted in every person who needed healing being completely healed. Likewise, in my gathering, the Holy Spirit went before us and waited in anticipation for us to cross the threshold into the meeting space. As each woman entered the room, within seconds she either burst into tears, fell gently to the floor, or both as she encountered the presence of the Holy Spirit. His manifest presence, His glory, did adhere to us in a deeper way after we were prayed for at the conference, and we saw the stunning results.

God longingly desires to reveal numerous facets and dimensions of His glory to us. More than just a distant theological truth that we read about in the Bible, the glory of

God is a reality He invites us to investigate and experience. In every modern-day encounter with the glory of God, we find the Holy Spirit, who is seeking an intimate friendship with us. This is the central idea behind one aspect of glory known as the Shekinah glory.

What Is the Shekinah Glory?

Jewish rabbis created an expression to describe one aspect of God's glory. Although the word *shekinah* is not found in the Bible, its root word in the Hebrew shows us that His glory "dwells" with us.[2] Commentator Tony Garland explains that "whenever the invisible God becomes visible, and whenever the omnipresence of God is localized," *that* is the Shekinah glory.[3] As I explained in chapter 1, God is omnipresent, meaning He is everywhere all at the same time, yet He has chosen to dwell with His people and manifest His presence in certain locations throughout history.

We see the concept of the Shekinah glory displayed in mankind's earliest communion with the Lord. Both Adam and Eve "heard the sound of the LORD God as He was walking in the garden in the cool of the day" (Genesis 3:8). This shows us how He was both visible and centralized in the Garden of Eden and could interact with them.

We see another display of the Shekinah glory when the Israelites escaped Egypt on the route to Succoth. "By day the LORD went ahead of them in a pillar of cloud to guide them on their way and by night in a pillar of fire to give them light, so that they could travel by day or night" (Exodus 13:21). Wherever the Shekinah is, there is also the notion of His abiding and intimate presence. Here in the wilderness, the Lord was always before the Israelites, leading them to safety by His Shekinah glory.

When Solomon built and dedicated the beautifully ornate temple, he made a desperate plea before the Lord: "Will God really dwell on earth with humans?" (2 Chronicles 6:18). How did the Lord respond? He responded with His Shekinah glory. His glory fell like fire from heaven and consumed the burnt offering and sacrifices being offered to Him and then filled the temple in the form of a powerful cloud. This cloud of glory was so overwhelming that the priests could not immediately enter the temple (see 2 Chronicles 7:1–3). The Lord was saying through these acts of glory, *I've come to dwell with you.*

God's Glory Brings Growth and Renewal

In August 1999, the Holy Spirit invaded our weekly prayer service in a unique way. Ron and I had just returned home from a conference at the International Church of Las Vegas. While there, we had received a special prayer of impartation for greater ministry from the conference speakers, much like I had described earlier with Randy Clark. I specifically remember guest speaker Dr. James Moracco, senior pastor of Kings Cathedral in Maui, praying over Ron and me and then prophesying by the unction of the Spirit, "Your church will grow!" We felt the glory of God as this took place, and I fell to the floor with what began as a deep belly laugh that continued for at least thirty minutes. Some refer to this manifestation of glory as "holy laughter," and I would clarify the experience from the Bible as being "joy inexpressible and full of glory" (1 Peter 1:8 NKJV).

When we returned home, Ron and I attended our weekly prayer service like normal—but that night was far from normal. The atmosphere of the room was electric. You could sense the activity of God and the presence of His holy angels charging the atmosphere. During the church services the next day, there was a genuine move of the Holy Spirit for the first time in the two years we had been pastoring there. People flooded the altars, tears streaming down their faces, all of them wanting more of the power of God. This was the beginning of renewal in our church, but there were some immediate challenges. (When I use the term *renewal*, I am referring to manifestations of the Holy Spirit: speaking in tongues, prophecy, supernatural healings, miracles, etc.)

Somewhere along the way, the more established, seasoned group of Christians in our fellowship had developed a short-sighted paradigm for renewal and revival. Based on their personal experiences, they could accept a visitation of God's glory for our church as long as it was temporary. They could not, however, accept a continuous habitation of His presence. We realized soon enough through their side snipes and blatant complaints that this particular group was waiting for the move of God to end. They clearly wanted their dead, religious routines back.

Ron and I knew in our hearts that God had come to dwell with us. He was not just passing by. We shifted how we ministered during the Sunday services with that truth in mind, and we painfully watched entire families leave our church to find more traditional and predictable environments. All the time, we kept a firm hold on Dr. Moracco's prophetic word: "Your church will grow!" That word, thankfully, has come to pass, and we have grown numerically, seeing renewal and revival ever since.

A Glory Cloud Carries God's Presence

One manifestation of the Shekinah glory can be seen in the form of a cloud. Unlike the atmospheric clouds above us, this cloud is a supernatural and physical manifestation of the presence of the Lord. As I described earlier, it was a distinguishable cloud of glory in the sky above that led the Israelites through the wilderness. It was a distinguishable cloud that surrounded Mount Sinai, the place where the Israelites broke covenant with God through worship of the golden calf. This same glory cloud also settled upon and filled the tent of meeting, also known as the tabernacle of Moses, and then later came and filled Solomon's temple. The tent of meeting was an actual tent that served as a temporary meeting place primarily between God and Moses as he sojourned with the Israelites in the wilderness. It was a precursor to the more permanent temple in Jerusalem. Although the glory cloud was specifically described in just the Old Testament, many will still attest that the manifestation has not passed away with the New Testament.

Have you ever seen the presence of God's glory in the form of a cloud? I have never seen this myself, but I know several people who have. They often describe it as a white mist or a cloud that comes in the form of thick, dense "sparkles."

During a time of fasting and prayer, Michelle Muscarella, who described herself as a busy single mom of one fantastic daughter, was praying with her three friends when she was suddenly surrounded by brilliant blue luminescent sparkles. She said the colorful lights were "alive" and moved all around her and then they were gone.

Michelle Morse, a social worker for very at-risk children in Central California, attended a conference at Bethel Church in Redding, California, where a glory cloud appeared in the church's main sanctuary.[4] She, and others, became surrounded by an actual cloud, then she noticed that her hands had flecks of gold on them. "The presence of God and His overwhelming love felt so strong in that moment that I could not stop crying," she said. "The cloud definitely carried His tangible presence, and I sat there for several minutes just weeping in the midst of it."

Minister and Author Jeff Jansen also experienced the cloud of glory, but in a much stronger dimension. Jeff held a miracle crusade in Seoul, Korea, with six thousand people in attendance. When the cloud of glory came into the atmosphere of that crusade, he described what happened: "Miracle after staggering miracle took place each night. People brought in on mats would walk out healed. Countless blind and deaf individuals were completely healed. Tumors dissolved and legs grew out all because of the atmospheric glory of God that hovered in and around the building." He could see as well as "feel" the cloud of glory.[5]

These are just a few modern-day examples of the Shekinah glory of God in the form of a distinguishable cloud. Behind the awe and wonder of this experience, however, is still the understanding that He has come to dwell with us. He has not come to simply visit us and move on. Many people focus on the miracle of the cloud, or perhaps the fire or brilliant lights, but then neglect or misunderstand the message behind the Shekinah presence of God. He has come to abide with us in intimate fellowship. He is drawing our hearts close to His.

Still the struggle to find that level of relationship can be altogether real, and historically so. There developed tremendous strife between God and the Israelites because God was and is always perfectly holy and the Israelites were perfectly not. They would not follow His commandments and kept worshiping other gods. Yet He desired and pursued the most intimate of all relationships with His people, even referring to Himself as Israel's husband (see Jeremiah 31:32; Isaiah 54:5; Hosea 2:7). Later, unfortunately, He divorced the entire nation of Israel due to her "harlotries," meaning He turned completely away from the nation for worshiping other gods besides Him (see Jeremiah 3:1, 8). Despite their messy divorce, God was determined to find a way to be with His people, and so a new form of the Shekinah glory emerged in the New Testament in the form of Jesus Christ.

Jesus Is the New Shekinah Glory

How was the incarnation of Jesus a new form of the Shekinah glory? When I mention the incarnation, I am referring to Jesus, the Son of God, taking on the form of human flesh. Again, the core concept behind the Shekinah glory is that the invisible God has been made visible and He has come to dwell with us. We read this about Him: "The Word became flesh and made his dwelling among us. We have seen his glory, the glory of the one and only Son, who came from the Father, full of grace and truth" (John 1:14). In the original Greek, the word *dwelling* in this passage means "to pitch tent, encamp; to tabernacle, dwell in a tent."[6]

Moses did something similar in the wilderness with the Israelites. He pitched a tent, known as the tabernacle of meeting, then God's brilliant glory descended from heaven to rest upon it. At the tabernacle in the wilderness, Moses and the Israelites could meet with and behold the glory of the Lord, which continued with the more permanent temple later in Jerusalem. Sadly, Israel's harlotries and abominations finally drove His Shekinah presence completely out of Solomon's temple. The Israelites learned way too late that the Shekinah glory had protected and preserved them from their merciless enemies. Once the glory left, they were taken captive by the Babylonians, their beautiful temple was decimated, and God stopped speaking to them for four hundred years, until John the Baptist.[7]

Young's Literal Translation describes John 1:14 a little differently than the other translations: "And the Word became flesh, and did *tabernacle* among us" (emphasis added). Some believe the word *tabernacle* adds a much richer meaning to what Jesus did on earth than the word *dwell*.[8] The tabernacle in the Old Testament demonstrated God's abiding Shekinah presence, but it also pointed to an even more glorious future, a future that introduced substantial reconciliation between God and man. Our heavenly Father began to speak and call His people back to Him as He had prophesied centuries before through the prophet Hosea: "But then I will win her back once again. I will lead her into the desert and speak tenderly to her there" (Hosea 2:14 NLT). Communication between God and man reemerged through John the Baptist, and the Shekinah glory reappeared with Jesus, illuminated through many signs and wonders.

Being fully God and fully man, Jesus did an astonishing thing while on the earth. He laid aside His divine privileges and chose to live among us as a man without sin, but anointed and passionately led by the Spirit of glory. I think this passage brings us clarity: "Who, being in very nature God, did not consider equality with God something to be used to his own advantage; rather, he made himself nothing by taking the very nature of a servant, being made in human likeness" (Philippians 2:6–7). Jesus then taught us by personal example how to authentically live as a glory carrier on the earth.

The Holy Spirit Is Gentle and Fierce

Jesus' ministry began with a personalized Holy Spirit encounter. While He was baptized in water by John the Baptist, all four Gospel accounts describe how the Holy Spirit descended upon Him from heaven like a dove. The Spirit of glory is portrayed as a dove because He has a deeply gentle nature, and this was a tender moment between Father, Son and Spirit. It was so raw and tender that our heavenly Father was compelled to express His unfathomable affirmation before the crowds: "And a voice from heaven said, 'This is my Son, whom I love; with him I am well pleased'" (Matthew 3:17).

The apostle Mark is the only one who writes that the Holy Spirit shifts from gentle dove to something fiercer after Jesus' baptism and heavenly endorsement: "Immediately the Spirit drove Him into the wilderness. And He was there in the wilderness forty days, tempted by Satan, and was with the wild beasts; and the angels ministered to Him" (Mark 1:12–13 NKJV). The word for "drove" here in the Greek (*ekballō*, which means to cast out, drive out or expel)[9] is the same word employed in the driving out of demons (Mark 1:34, 39).[10] Some Bible teachers strongly emphasize how the Holy Spirit is a gentleman, and rightfully so, but at the same time He is not skittish or weak, nor does He tiptoe around us. We read that "the mature children of God are those who are moved by the impulses of the Holy Spirit" (Romans 8:14 TPT). In our teachings about the Holy Spirit, we should not then reduce Him to someone we can manage or feel in control of. He is both gentle and fierce, and as glory carriers we are to be led by Him in the fullness of His expression.

Throughout the gospels and tucked in between miracles, we see the Son of Man[11] engaged in passionate dialogue with almighty God. He was so prayerful and powerful that His disciples urged Him to instruct them how to pray, too. We can see why. Beginning with His first public prayer immediately following His water baptism, we read that when He prayed, heaven opened and the Holy Spirit came upon Him (see Luke 3:21–22). Here He was officially anointed by the Holy Spirit for ministering in signs and wonders, which are clear demonstrations of glory. He cast out demons, healed the sick and raised the dead, all the while calling people into repentance and back into relationship with God.

Later Jesus revealed that He did nothing on His own; He did only what He saw the Father doing (see John 5:19). What exactly does that mean? I believe the Holy Spirit was giving Jesus visions while He prayed, specifically glimpses, images and internal movies to show Him where to go each day and what to do. In John 14:12 He declared, "Whoever believes in me will do the works I have been doing, and they will do even greater things than these, because I am going to the Father."

What began with the Spirit can only continue in the Spirit. We, too, can step into a new form of Shekinah glory because we have been made a temple of the Holy Spirit. As I mentioned in chapter 1, He dwells within us and turns our physical bodies into a home. The implications of this truth are mind-blowing. Have you considered His habitation in your life? And that the Holy Spirit will speak to you in visions as you pray as He did with Jesus? The Spirit of glory wants to partner with you with signs and wonders—His signpost to a dying world that He has come to dwell with us.

We Are Temples of the Holy Spirit

The apostle Paul asked the believers in Corinth, who were engaging in sexual sin much like the pagans around them: "Do you not know that he who unites himself with a prostitute is one with her in body? For it is said, 'The two will become one flesh.' But whoever is united with the Lord is one with him in spirit" (1 Corinthians 6:16–17). To unite yourself either to a prostitute or the Lord means to be glued, cemented and fastened together.[12] Paul then posed another thought-provoking question: "Do you not know that your bodies are temples of the Holy Spirit?" (v. 19). That is strong imagery, but a glory carrier wholeheartedly leans into and cleaves to the Spirit of God. The miracles, which are displays of glory, are then the outward manifestations of that yielded heart union.

At a prophetic gathering in Australia, I began to teach about dream interpretation and how God speaks to us more often than not in our dreams. I also shared my personal testimony and how I learned that night terrors, insomnia and struggles in the night are often an assignment from hell to disrupt your dream life, a key realm where we hear the voice of God. After my time of teaching, I invited people to raise their hands if they needed prayer to sleep better at night. When half of the room raised their hands, I was suddenly caught in an unusual spiritual battle. I whispered to my intercessors in the front row, "I'm really fighting with something right now." Remember that those who cleave to the Spirit of glory will display His Shekinah glory. We will do the works of Jesus and even greater.

My first attempt to pray was just a general prayer over the crowd since there were so many in need. "Heavenly Father, in the name of Jesus, I command Your people to be loosed from night terrors, torments, nightmares and sleeplessness." I did not feel the release that I was expecting, so I began laying hands on people right in their seats and commanding their deliverance. I felt the fierce, determined presence of the Holy Spirit, then a spiritual "bomb" went off in the room. All of a sudden, many people screamed and groaned as demons left them. Some physically convulsed as they were set free; others slithered like snakes. The ministry teams and I spent a lot of time that night praying and lovingly ministering to those needing new realms of freedom. I honestly did not know what I was walking into that night, but I followed God's lead and we all experienced the results.

The glory of God, the visible and miraculous manifestation of His presence, is highly multifaceted in its nature and expression. I believe that as we go from glory to glory, expressions of His glory, such as the Shekinah and others, will continue to unfold in dimensions we never thought possible.

Does this fill you with anticipation as much as it does me? Are you ready for more? Another unusual realm of glory, known as the kabad glory, is weighty and has the power to transform you into a spiritual heavyweight. This is the topic of my next chapter.

KINGDOM PRINCIPLES

1. Jewish rabbis created an expression to describe one aspect of God's glory. Although the word *shekinah* is not found in the Bible, its root word in the Hebrew shows us what it does, specifically that His glory "dwells" with us.

2. The idea behind the Shekinah glory is displayed in mankind's earliest communion with the Lord. Both Adam and Eve "heard the sound of the Lord God as He was walking in the garden in the cool of the day" (Genesis 3:8). Wherever the Shekinah is, there is also the notion of His abiding and intimate presence.

3. One manifestation of the Shekinah glory can be seen in the form of a cloud. Unlike the atmospheric clouds

above us, this cloud is a supernatural and physical manifestation of the presence of the Lord. Many attest that the manifestation of the Holy Spirit has not passed away with the New Testament.

4. Many people focus on the miracle of the cloud, or perhaps the fire or brilliant lights, but then neglect or misunderstand the message behind the Shekinah presence of God. He has come to abide with us in intimate fellowship. He is drawing our hearts close to His.

5. Because of Israel's idolatry, the Shekinah glory departed from the temple and God was silent for four hundred years. A new form of the Shekinah glory emerged in the New Testament in the form of Jesus Christ, illuminated through many signs and wonders.

THOUGHTS FOR REFLECTION

1. Have you ever experienced the Shekinah glory in the form of a cloud or in another way? If so, how did that impact you?

2. Encounters with God's glory not only display His greatness but invite us into deeper relationship. God is not showing off; He is saying, *I've come to dwell with you.* Does that change how you look at miracles when you encounter them?

3. Jesus modeled for us the lifestyle of a glory carrier, beginning with the Holy Spirit descending upon Him like a dove and continuing through a passionate lifestyle of prayer. Are you beginning to seek out the Holy Spirit? Are you engaging the Holy Spirit in the place of prayer?

4. The Holy Spirit is both gentle and fierce, and as glory carriers we are to be led by Him in the fullness of His expression. Have you, then, accepted ideas that reduce the Holy Spirit to someone you can manage or control?

5. Outward manifestations of glory in the form of signs and wonders are a reflection of your relationship with the Holy Spirit. Does this frustrate you or encourage you? (It is normal if your answer is "both.")

4

The Kabad Glory

My first year as a Christian was amazing. For the first time in my life, I felt genuinely happy. There was peace in my home, and we were growing in our faith in Christ as a family. I was also learning about prayer, my favorite subject, and enjoying the fellowship of my new Christian friends. Things were going so well that I had no clue my faith would soon be challenged by Satan. After I had been a Christian for a year, I became more and more troubled. Even though I was faithfully growing in spiritual disciplines (i.e., going to church, praying, reading the Bible, etc.), I had lost those initial feelings of happiness and peace. In addition, I began sensing dark things—an evil spirit, to be exact—as if revisiting demonic encounters I had only experienced before becoming a Christian.

Things finally came to a head at a house prayer service, one I had been attending for less than a year with a neighbor. Toward the end of our time in prayer, one of the women in attendance looked at me and described how she could see a spirit of sorcery standing over me. When she said that, something picked me up and threw me against the wall. Next, I experienced one of the worst demonic manifestations I have personally witnessed in all my days of ministry. I wrote about this incident in more detail in my book *The Intercessors Handbook* (Chosen, 2016). The women at the prayer meeting were unable to lead me into freedom either.

I was tormented by this demon for around three months until one day, by the prompting of the Holy Spirit, I said this: "I will never serve you. I will only serve Jesus Christ." At my command, the demon left and never returned, and I gained a newfound spiritual authority. Through this experience, I learned from the Holy Spirit how to have spiritual authority for myself and that God is bigger than the devil. My deliverance from spiritual bondage left a desire in me to see others be free of their spiritual issues, especially in the areas of the occult, fear and torment.

My Introduction into "Heavyweight" Deliverance

After my husband and I became pastors, I began focusing on research and study, along with prayer, to develop an effective deliverance ministry within our church. Although definitions and methods can vary, deliverance ministry involves the process of breaking intentional and unintentional agreements with demons that give them legal rights to oppress our lives. Once these agreements are broken, we are authorized to cast them out in the name of Jesus (see Mark 16:17).[1] I recognized early on in ministry that too many Christians were saved and going to heaven when they died, but like me, they were still bound by demonic forces. They needed a loving but effective process to bring them out of spiritual captivity.

Naturally speaking, we often talk about people being heavyweights in terms of influence and authority, but weightiness can include spiritual influence and authority as well. One of the leaders I most respect in deliverance ministry is an evangelist from Argentina by the name of Carlos Annacondia. Carlos was a highly successful businessman who gave his life to Jesus at age thirty-five. Five days after receiving Christ into his heart, he experienced the Spirit of glory like a burning fire and received his supernatural prayer language. "At that moment, I felt His fire all over me! I was shaking and began to speak in my heavenly language," he told Premier Christian Radio. "Almost immediately, things began to happen. People felt burning electricity come out of my hands and demons began manifesting in those around me. I didn't know what any of this was."[2]

After this transformational encounter, he went on to become a glory carrier of the heavy kind. He felt an intensely deep cry from the Holy Spirit within his own spirit for revival in Argentina, a cry that moved him to tears and wailing, including deep intercession. Compelled by the Spirit, he began to minister the message of salvation in small towns and venues before surrendering his prosperous business to the Lord to become a full-time evangelist. This resulted in a powerful soul-winning ministry marked by signs and wonders, the most distinct sign being the ministry of mass deliverance. Many believers engage in deliverance ministry, but Carlos transformed from humble evangelist into a heavyweight deliverance minister when he encountered the kabad glory of God.

At his services and crusades, Annacondia would often rebuke the demons that had oppressed and bound the attendees with this command, "*¡Oíme bien, Satanás! ¡Fuera!*" (Listen to me, Satan! Out!). At his rebuke hundreds, and sometimes thousands, would then convulse and manifest demonically. His ministry teams would locate these individuals in the crowds, walk or carry them out to a designated ministry area, then lead them through a process of deliverance. The process of deliverance often involved repentance for specific sins that opened the doors to give demons access to their lives, after which the oppressing spirits could be cast out in Jesus' name.[3] I, too, desired to have this anointing of the Spirit to "set the oppressed free" (Luke 4:18) in greater measure so I could minister more effectively to others.

My husband and I decided to attend a conference in Florida where Carlos was ministering in order to learn more about deliverance ministry and to receive a prayer of impartation. During the conference, we were invited to a private ministers' luncheon where Carlos would teach and then pray for each of us to receive more of the Spirit's anointing. When the time came, we were asked to stand up and form a single-file line in the front of the room near the platform.

As Carlos began to walk slowly down the line, laying his hands on each person and praying for them, the presence of God was so heavy, I was unable to stand and fell backward onto the floor. I was quite aware that Carlos was approaching soon and I might not be prayed for as long as I remained on the ground. Somewhat frantic, I called out to the people standing around me, "Get me up! Get me up! I don't want to miss being prayed for!" It took three men, including my husband, to stand me up because a kind of glory came upon me that seemed to add weight to my then 125-pound frame.

Soon enough, Carlos laid hands on both my husband and me and prayed for us. All I remember is falling back to the floor once again under the heavy glory of the Holy Spirit. It has been years since this occurred, but deliverance ministry and intercession have grown to become the Spirit's strongest ministries through my life. I attribute this, in part, to this moment of encounter with the weighty, heavy glory of God.

Defining the Kabad Glory

In the previous chapter, we discussed one aspect of glory, the Shekinah glory, which is the visible manifestation of the presence of God that also hosts a heavenly message: He has come to dwell with us. In this chapter, we will look at another aspect of glory, the kabad glory or "heavy" glory of God.[4] First, let's look at the general use of the word *kabad*.

The literal meaning of *kabad* is "weighty" or "heavy."[5] For example, Moses' hands became heavy (*kabad*) in battle (see Exodus 17:12); there was a heavy (*kabad*) famine in the land (see Genesis 12:10); and the king's heavy (*kabad*) yoke became too burdensome (see 1 Kings 12:4). God's glory can also manifest in a heavy way. The priests were unable to stand because the heavy glory of God filled the temple (see 2 Chronicles 5:14), and in a negative sense, God's hand was heavy against the people of Ekron (see 1 Samuel 5:11).

We can also understand the word *kabad* by how it is joined with other words in the more poetical passages of the Bible. One commentator wrote,

> In Psalm 3:3, for example, the *kavod* of *Elohiym* (God) is paralleled with his "shield" and in Job 29:20, Job's *kavod* is paralleled with his "bow." In Psalm 24:8 we read "who is this king of the *kavod*, YHWH is strong and mighty, YHWH is mighty in battle." The original concrete meaning of *kavod* is battle armaments. The meaning "armament" fits with the literal meaning of the root of *kavod*, which is "heavy," and armaments are the heavy weapons and defenses of battle.[6]

Finally, the word *kabad* can be about the weight of a person's reputation, including God's reputation, and can be used figuratively to denote splendor, abundance, honor or glory.[7] For example, Abram was rich (*kabad*) in livestock (Genesis 13:2); God will honor (*kabad*) those who honor Him (1 Samuel 2:30); and David said he will glorify (*kabad*) the name of God forever (Psalm 86:12).

We have discussed how one must have a deep and consistent devotion to the Spirit of glory to be an effectual glory carrier. This is an intimate partnership, and we each have a unique part to play in this amazing relationship. At the same time, God will sovereignly manifest His glory when He wants to and how He wants to for His own purposes. For this reason, many have experienced the kabad glory quite by surprise and have never been the same again.

We see such an encounter in the life of the apostle Paul. While on a religious crusade against the Lord's disciples, he was confronted by the glory of God on the road to Damascus. This glory came in the form of an intense light from heaven, but I believe this light also contained His heavy glory. It was so heavy that it knocked Paul to the ground, and he was blinded for three days until he was supernaturally healed. This encounter transformed him from a persecutor of the early Church into a believer in Christ who carried and demonstrated the heavy kabad glory of God. This gained him a reputation for having spiritual authority not only with the Church at large but with Jewish exorcists and the invisible realm.

For example, seven sons of Sceva, a Jewish chief priest, attempted to cast a demon out of a man using the name of Jesus "whom Paul preaches" (Acts 19:13–14). In other words, they were not believers in Jesus but recognized the weight of Jesus' name during exorcisms and brazenly invoked His name to cast out spirits. Imagine that! On one occasion, these seven brash men were caught off guard when a demon answered them through a man being exorcised, saying, "Jesus I know, and Paul I know about, but who are you?" (v. 15). This man then overpowered all seven of them, beating them so badly until they all ran out of the house both naked and bleeding (see v. 16). The glory Paul carried was so heavy that even the demons knew his name.

A Heavy Glory for a Heavy Calling

When my husband and I first began leading Harvest Christian Center in Turlock, California, we had connected relationally with the International Church of Las Vegas and began attending conferences there quite regularly. During these special conferences, Senior Leaders Paul and Denise Goulet often brought the visiting ministers up to the front of the room just to pray for them and to encourage them in their ministry assignments. I became perplexed, actually embarrassed, when something kept happening to me as a direct result of these times of prayer.

The Goulets would enthusiastically call all of us ministers to the front of the room and sometimes even up to the platform. Next, they would physically lay their hands on us one by one while praying quite fervently. Before being released back to their seats, many received deeply from the Holy Spirit in response, even exhibiting a genuine manifestation, such as shaking, laughing or being "slain in the Spirit" (when you supernaturally fall to the ground, overwhelmed by the power of the Spirit, usually after being prayed for and having hands laid on you).[8] I, too, received deeply from the Spirit, but something much stronger seemed to happen to me in those moments. Remember that God will manifest

His glory when He wants to and how He wants to for His purposes.

During these times of ministry, I encountered the kabad glory of God. His presence sovereignly came upon me so heavily that I could not lift myself off the floor. It felt as if my entire being had been weighted down. This happened to me at least four times within a two- or three-year period at this church. And each time this happened, they would kindly leave me on the floor, wherever I landed, and move on with their services. The reason I was embarrassed was that I was consistently and conspicuously glued to the ground in front of their entire audience, and even once on their platform.

The Holy Spirit finally explained this to me. You see, I was a back-row kind of person all my life. I did not like to be seen and preferred to remain out of view, especially in front of a group or a crowd. Yet He left me in His heavy glory quite visibly and up front at these church services for a purpose. He was saying to me, *I didn't call you to be in the back or to be invisible. I called you to the front, and you will be seen by the masses.*

Is this a feeling or attitude that you can relate to? Are you called of God to lead and be in front of people, but instead you have remained a back-row hider? Are you sensing the presence of the Lord as you read this? If so, I encourage you to receive it as a sign that this instruction was not just for me, but an instruction from the Spirit for you as well. My prayer for you is, "More, Lord!"

A heavy calling is an automatic invitation to encounters with His heavy glory, something He will initiate sovereignly in your life at the right place and right time. This is a deeply transforming glory that supernaturally shapes you into an influencer and a glory carrier of the heavy kind. I have learned to pay attention to this kind of glory when I see people come under its weight. I know that something heavy is happening to them, but for a purpose.

It is important not to rush these moments, because God's deeper work takes time. "Some people want to get up too quickly," wrote Carol Arnott in the book *Preparing for the Glory*. "Of course God can work quickly, and He often does. But so many times, people get embarrassed or self-conscious and they want to get up before God is done with them. I tell them, 'No, you're not getting up. More, Lord. Fire on you.'"[9]

Healed in the Kabad Glory

The kabad glory is also a healing glory. It will heal your body and your mind. To clarify, there is a difference between the anointing for healing and experiencing the glory that results in healing. When you are one who operates in the anointing for healing, people often put a demand on it by faith, and it will flow out of you like a river to heal another person. Jesus experienced this when the woman with the issue of blood touched His robes, and He asked His disciples, "Who touched me? . . . Someone touched me; I know that power has gone out from me" (John 8:45–46).

Operating in the anointing for healing (or anointing for deliverance and miracles, etc.) can be physically draining because the physical body is involved. I have experienced this personally and have needed to stop ministering after a certain point, having become too physically drained. When God releases His heavy kabad glory, however, it is all Him. You do not feel drained because you are not involved. You can minister in His glory and still remain refreshed and strengthened.

During one of our required Bible courses at Oral Roberts University, I recall how our theology professor was doing his best to prepare the hundred or more students for an upcoming exam. There was only one amazing problem. The Holy Spirit began to fall heavily upon the students while he lectured. You could see and hear around the room the several *bumps* and *thuds* as the students both gracefully, and not so gracefully, slid out of their chairs onto the floor in fits of glorious laughter.

By the way, this type of encounter was happening all over the campus in response to the ministry of evangelist Rodney Howard-Browne in 1993. He carried an unusual glory that resulted in deep transformation for those who received his ministry. Students testified about receiving deep inner healing, physical healing and an overall increase of joy, just to name a few. I recall that when he walked near you, you could feel something heavy and powerful radiating off his person. This was the Holy Spirit; it was His glory, but it was weighty in substance. I have testified about this experience many times over the years. What is amazing is that when I share about it, even after all this time, there is a release of glory that takes place. I have seen many people step into the same experience of healing and joy, much like we did back then, just by hearing the story.

Linda Downey, a nurse and lover of world missions, experienced a physical healing after she had an encounter with the heavy glory. She said, "After a severe case of pancreatitis in 2012, I was left with pancreatic insufficiency. I had to take pancreatic enzymes in order to digest any of my food. In 2016 at a large prayer meeting at Harvest Christian Center in Turlock, California, I felt the glory of God fall as we were worshiping and praying. I then heard the Lord speak to me that He had healed me of my pancreatic insufficiency. I knew that I had heard Him clearly, and I was so filled with joy and the weight of His presence."

She continued, "The next morning, I eagerly took my first meal without my enzymes waiting to see if the severe pain started because it always would about thirty minutes after my meal. That was two years ago and I've never had any pain since. I have been able to eat anything I want and I have never had to take another pancreatic enzyme. God's glory healed me instantly!"

Another woman, Kim Wright, described a life-changing healing with the unexpected release of the kabad kind of glory. She shared, "When I gave my life to Christ, I was very sick. A doctor told me that I had arthritis in my rib cage along with having bronchitis and that I would eventually end up in a wheelchair due to the arthritis. I went to a church meeting in a small town near my home. When the evangelist laid his hands on me and prayed, I was slain so heavily in the Spirit that I didn't move for twenty minutes or so. When I finally got up, I was completely healed with no cough, no pain, no anything."

Lisa Lei-Sure, a business owner, wife and mother, was healed emotionally after encountering the kabad glory during an Outpouring service also at Harvest Christian Center. "Last year, Jennifer Eivaz was teaching and then called us up to lay hands on us and pray for God to heal our emotions, broken hearts and turmoil, etc. As she laid her hands upon my head, I fell to the ground under a heavy presence of the Lord. For a few minutes, I just felt peaceful. Then as I sat up, I felt invisible hands on my shoulders gently pushing me back down. Next, I felt a strong, bubbly feeling and began laughing uncontrollably. Once more I tried to sit up, only to be pushed down again. I am not sure how long this went on, but when I did get up I was drunk in the Spirit. A few days later while having a conversation with my sister, I realized I could talk about my dad without cringing or being sarcastic or getting angry. God miraculously healed my broken heart!"

Accessing the Kabad Glory

Now that we know what the kabad glory is, that it is a heavy glory, and a kind of glory that God releases sovereignly for His purposes, the next question you might have is, *How, then, do I access it?* Although there is no formula or methodology for experiencing the heavy glory of God, here are a few suggestions to help you:

1. Continue to cultivate a relationship with the Holy Spirit.

Being in a growing relationship with the Spirit of glory marks you for these kinds of glory encounters. Just remember, however, that the Holy Spirit will never be prostituted for His treasury of glory. We read, "Blessed are the pure in heart, for they will see God" (Matthew 5:8). We always approach the Holy Spirit with a pure heart and with a pure agenda. Nevertheless, the pure in heart will see Him, and I believe the pure in heart will experience His kabad glory, too.

2. Ask for it.

Jesus said, "If you remain in me and my words remain in you, ask whatever you wish, and it will be done for you" (John 15:7). We are encouraged to ask. Not only to ask, but to ask whatever we wish. The qualifier, however, is that we remain in Him and in His Word.

3. Be in proximity of those who demonstrate the kabad glory.

There are some people that seem to walk in the kabad glory and minister out of it on a regular basis. Being in proximity with such persons certainly puts you in proximity of the heavy anointing that they carry. Author and minister Jeff Jansen and

I were conversing on the set of *Sid Roth's It's Supernatural!* television program. He and I both shared a common experience, one reflecting a person who walks in the heavy glory. Whenever and wherever we minister, people are consistently slain in the Spirit, among other things. I recognize this does not happen with everyone, but at the same time I do not want to appear boastful either. I cannot make that happen without the Holy Spirit, but the manifestations we see are a by-product of the heavy glory that we both walk in. Those who are in proximity of us will most likely encounter Him in that manner.

My prayer for you right now is that your hunger would deepen for weighty encounters with His glory, that you would begin to seek Him more and more with eager expectation. At the same time, as a glory carrier, recognize the weighty assignment knowing you will need to cultivate a heart and mindset of a finisher. Remember the words of the apostle Paul: "I have fought the good fight, I have finished the race, I have kept the faith" (2 Timothy 4:7). A glory carrier inevitably faces persecution and suffering. Jesus made this comment to His disciples: "Remember what I told you: 'A servant is not greater than his master.' If they persecuted me, they will persecute you also" (John 15:20). This is the high price to be paid for knowing and encountering the Holy Spirit and beautifully evolving from glory to glory. I want to encourage you, a glory carrier, to not ever retreat—no matter what it costs. A unique, glorious encounter of supernatural love awaits you, one that will sustain your heart and create a finisher out of you.

KINGDOM PRINCIPLES

1. The kabad glory is weighty in nature and highly transforming, and it can turn you into a spiritual heavyweight.

2. To be an effectual glory carrier requires a deep and consistent devotion to the Spirit of glory. At the same time, God will sovereignly manifest His glory when He wants to and how He wants to for His own purposes.

3. A heavy calling is an invitation into encounters with His heavy glory, something He will initiate sovereignly in your life at the right place and right time. This is a deeply transforming glory, and something that supernaturally shapes you into an influencer and a glory carrier of the heavy kind.

4. When the kabad glory comes upon you, you will often feel supernaturally weighted down, even glued to the ground. It is important not to rush these moments because God's deeper work takes time. Do not get up too quickly because you are embarrassed or self-conscious.

5. The kabad glory is also a healing glory. It will heal your body and your mind. It is different than the anointing for healing.

THOUGHTS FOR REFLECTION

1. Have you ever encountered the kabad glory of God? How did you know?

2. Shaking, laughing, falling to the ground in the glory—why do people have physical reactions to the glory of God? When is it real and when is it fake?

3. Do physical reactions to His manifest presence embarrass you personally? Would you prefer to not have that happen to you? Why or why not?

4. Are you called of God to lead people in some way, but find yourself staying behind or out of view? The kabad

glory turns people like you from back-row hiders into heavyweight influencers. Do you then, as Carol Arnott wrote, need more "fire on you!"?

5. Is it time to pray a bolder and more dangerous prayer: "Heavenly Father, we ask You to release Your kabad glory!"?

5

No Guts, No Glory

I was on my way to Bangkok, Thailand, on an intercessory assignment with a small team, but first planned a stop in Perth, Australia, to minister at a prayer conference. I became strangely ill a few weeks prior to this trip and ended up in the emergency room, unable to breathe, with a mysterious respiratory illness. The doctors could not pinpoint what it was, but still I was so ill that I could not get out of bed for five straight days. I suspected my illness was spiritually connected, but did not understand why. While resting and slowly recovering, I researched the history of Perth and was surprised to learn that its chief deity was a kind of python spirit known as a Wagyl.

Aboriginal tribes described the Wagyl as a snakelike dreamtime creature responsible for the creation and protection of the waterways and landforms around present-day Perth and the southwest of Western Australia. These tribes were later appointed as the guardians of the land by the Wagyl and certain tribal elders were visited by and would speak to this dreamtime being.[1] Although this could seem to be somewhat mythological, elements of the Wagyl are often represented in Perth architectural design structures.[2] And, in my experience, things we dismiss as myths are actually spiritual strongholds in the land that ultimately need our intercession.

Biblically, this spirit would be similar to the territorial demon that possessed the slave girl in Acts 16:16: "It happened that as we were going to the place of prayer, a slave-girl [possessed with] a spirit of divination met us, who was bringing her masters much profit by fortune-telling" (NASB). The spirit of divination referred to in this verse is actually a python spirit and historically believed to be the guardian spirit for the oracle of Delphi.[3] Think of how a python spirit behaves in the natural, and you will get the picture.

This spirit does a lot of evil things, but a few characteristics of this kind of attack against you are to squeeze the life out of you, suffocate you, constrict you, confine you and to tightly restrict you into a maddening frustration. It also fiercely attacks both prayer and the gift of prophecy, both of which are the antithesis of a python spirit because they breathe the life of God into people and places. I believe this is why the slave girl interrupted Paul and his companions on their way to prayer, and I believe this was the spiritual problem behind my physical inability to breathe.

Thankfully, I recovered enough to still take the long flight to Perth. While at Paradox Church, which by the way had cultivated the most unusual atmosphere of worship intimacy that I have ever encountered, it just seemed appropriate to teach and activate on prophetic intercession, spiritual warfare and the basic gift of prophecy in connection to intercession. There was an unusually high level of spiritual warfare connected with this territory, and I could fill a book with all the stories, but Jesus proved victorious every time. As much as this demonic stronghold resisted and buffeted me before, during and after, the Holy Spirit Himself had prepared an even more powerful encounter as well.

Here is what happened: The night after the final conference session, I was visited in the night by the Holy Spirit (see Psalm 17:3). In the strangest, but most tender way, He picked me up from my bed and brought me to His chest in a brief, but life-changing holy embrace. Upon contact, I felt something from Him drop into my heart, and I was completely undone by it. When I mention the heart, I am not talking about my heart as a vital organ, a muscle that pumps blood throughout the body. I am referring to the spiritual part of us where our emotions and desires dwell, something the Bible mentions almost three hundred times. The reason for becoming undone is that my heart was miraculously resuscitated by that encounter.

I did not recognize until that moment that large parts of my heart had died. It had died because of grief, pain, sorrow, loss, deep betrayal and so much more. I did this unconsciously, but I had killed off my own heart from too much pain and no longer had any feeling or care in those dead places. That is a very dangerous place to be, because you cannot be led by the Spirit in the places you no longer feel, see or care. This is why we are admonished, "Keep your heart with all diligence, for out of it spring the issues of life" (Proverbs 4:23 NKJV). I still had to go to work on all those places where I had experienced emotional heart failure with the help of Christian counseling and inner healing ministry, but through this encounter I had come to life again, and it was obvious to everyone around me.

I began to minister out of this experience in nearly every conference I had been invited to afterward, noticing the distinct connection between an awakened heart and a release of His glory. As I shared about the experience and prayed over people's hearts, they, too, began to have their own experiences. Their hearts awakened in the presence of His glory, and their hearts also resuscitated. People could feel again, care again and see the Lord again.

I remember listening to the powerful testimony of one older man whom I would describe as family-oriented, respectable and seasoned in the Lord. Crying, he held his hand over his heart. "I can feel it in here," he said. "He's healing my heart!" He was referring to a deep wound that involved his natural father. Still in tears, he then expressed his desire to travel and partner with organizations overseas that specifically helped orphaned children. By having his heart healed from a father wound, he was supernaturally released to be a father to the nations. That blessed me like nothing else, but there was still another piece to this journey that would test my heart and my obedience in order to finish a difficult intercessory assignment.

Just prior to ministering for the second time at Paradox Church, senior leaders Brad and Lisa Joss, their intercessors and later my prayer partners began sharing a similar thought being revealed to all of us by the Holy Spirit. The thought was to expect a travail, or a spiritual birth of some kind, at this upcoming conference, which meant He had plans to birth something new. To explain this concept better, travailing prayer is a prayer of the Spirit and a prayer without words. It really does feel like giving birth to something. Most people point to this verse for context, "In the same way, the Spirit helps us in our weakness. We do not know what we ought to pray for, but the Spirit himself intercedes for us through wordless groans" (Romans 8:26). You might groan or weep in depths that you cannot create on your own and for sure, it is a prayer that you cannot mimic or hype. Travailing prayer is a prayer of the Spirit, and a very powerful prayer that ushers in a new season, new ministry and more.

To make this even more dramatic, just a few weeks before this prophetic gathering took place, the Holy Spirit woke me at 3:00 a.m. and counseled me for two hours about the travail that I would experience while there. In short, He said, *You will enter into a hard travail while there, specifically a travail of heart. It will be very painful, and you will want to die to escape it. Tell their intercessory teams as well as your own to pray that you would not die.*

I had never heard of such a thing and was shocked at His words. By that time, however, I had learned to follow Him and obey even if I did not understand. I did what He told me to do, my teams were praying, and now we were just waiting upon Him. In addition, I was processing the intensity of this prophetic act, something He was requiring of me and still something that I might not live through because something about it was going to be so intense. I reminded myself that a glory carrier does not love his or her life more than death, and I felt His intense love for me at the same time. His love is what sustained me.

Now at the conference, I had just closed a private meeting with a small group of intercessors when everything He said beforehand did happen. I entered into a travail of heart by the Holy Spirit, meaning I could feel birth pains in the heart area of my physical body. It was deeply spiritual, but also physical and excruciatingly painful. It was so excruciating that I did not think I would make it to the end. Their intercessors faithfully prayed me through it, about a forty-five-minute process, and thankfully I am alive to tell the story. On my end, I was able to share somewhat in the sufferings of Christ, something that awakens an appreciation and love in you like nothing else can. On their end, in addition to moving from a small space into a much larger campus they are also experiencing clusters and bursts of new visitors every week at their regular Sunday services. All of these being signs of "new birth."

Although this experience is not typical, we have to settle it within our own hearts that a glory carrier cannot love their life more than death. There are assignments of glory that will require unusual courage. At the same time, we will not risk our lives for Him any further than we have encountered His love either. To be more accurate, it is not that we *will not* take the risk; we actually *cannot* as fear has too much of a grip on our hearts. Do you still want to be a glory carrier? Are you daunted by the possibilities of taking great risks? We learn from the life and death of Stephen in the Bible how to love Christ and people deeply, something that prioritizes our choices in extreme circumstances.

Chosen to Be an Outstanding Glory Carrier

In the early days of the Church, an unfortunate prejudice surfaced toward the Greek-speaking Jews, the Hellenists. Their widows were being ignored during the daily food distribution. These widows were fully Jewish, had come to faith in Christ and were part of the Church, but had lived in other Greek countries before coming to Israel.[4] They were in the minority and considered inferior, having been steeped too deeply in Greek culture and language.[5] When complaints arose by the foreign Jews, the apostles delegated the solution to the disciples.

So the Twelve gathered all the disciples together and said, "It would not be right for us to neglect the ministry of the word of God in order to wait on tables. Brothers and sisters, choose seven men from among you who are known to be full of the Spirit and wisdom. We will turn this responsibility over to them and will give our attention to prayer and the ministry of the word."

Acts 6:2–4

The church then chose the seven, but one of the men, Stephen, seemed to stand out more than the rest.

Stephen was an outstanding glory carrier. He radiated a life filled with the Holy Spirit and performed great signs and wonders among the people. Keep in mind that he was not an apostle or a prophet, but an ordinary man assigned by the church to help feed the widows. The Spirit's manifestation of signs and wonders through his life and given that he was a Christ follower garnered deathly opposition nonetheless. Envious men from the local synagogues produced false witnesses against Stephen, causing him to be arrested, put on trial, then sentenced to death. While being falsely accused, Stephen's face supernaturally and marvelously radiated with the glory of God in the presence of the entire Sanhedrin (see Acts 6:15). And then while being stoned to death, we read the stunning account of how Stephen "being full of the Holy Spirit and led by Him, gazed into heaven and saw the glory [the great splendor and majesty] of God, and Jesus standing at the right hand of God" (7:55 AMP).

Stephen had an undeniably impactful life. He was the first Christian martyr and the catalyst for the persecution that caused the scattering of the Church away from Jerusalem. Some believe this was in fulfillment of Jesus' words in Acts 1:8: "But you will receive power when the Holy Spirit comes on you; and you will be my witnesses in Jerusalem, and in all Judea and Samaria, and to the ends of the earth." It is doubtful that the Church would have dispersed unless a significant persecution had been launched against them.[6] Stephen, being led by the Spirit, uttered an inspired prayer at the moment of his death. "While they were stoning him, Stephen prayed, 'Lord Jesus, receive my spirit.' Then he fell on his knees and cried out, 'Lord, do not hold this sin against them.' When he had said this, he fell asleep" (7:59–60). Remember, he offered up this prayer—to not curse his enemies but to bless them instead—under an open heaven (see Luke 6:28).

Stephen's life reflected one who had cultivated a deep friendship with the Spirit of God. He emerged as a passionate risk taker for Jesus and was not afraid of death. Glory carriers do become unusual risk takers, but why they do this is often misunderstood. We love to read their stories of great exploits. Only God wants you to be the story now. The adage is true: no guts, no glory. But how does this authentically emerge in us today?

The Doxa Glory of God

We have looked at two words for glory in the Old Testament, *shekinah* and *kabad*, but there is another word for glory in the New Testament—the Greek word *doxa*, which carries a lot of the same meaning as kabad, such as the notion of reputation, splendor, abundance, honor, fame, majesty and magnificence. Again, like the word *kabad*, *doxa* is objective, and so the full meaning is determined by how it is applied to something. One commentator, in reference to human beings, described how both *kabad* and *doxa* are "the very character or noblest part of man."[7]

Guillermo Maldonado wrote in reference to God that "doxa speaks of the real majesty belonging to God as the

Supreme Governor—majesty in the sense of the absolute perfection of His deity. When referring to the Son, it alludes to the majestic royalty of the Messiah—this being the highest level of exaltation and the condition to which the Father raised Jesus after He fulfilled His purpose on earth, defeating Satan and death."[8]

God reveals His doxa glory to mankind through His manifest presence. By way of undeniable encounters with His glory, He then engages us in relationship. When God reveals His glory, because of His majestic nature, it is always compelling and dynamic and intended to create a response from those who witness it.[9] Those who respond are, then, those who supernaturally transform.

In Matthew 17, we read of an amazing encounter with God's glory. Right before the cross, Jesus was brilliantly transfigured in glory before Peter, James and John. We read, "There He was transfigured before them. His face shone like the sun, and his clothes became as white as the light" (Matthew 17:2). The word for "transfigured" in this verse is the Greek word *metamorphoo*, which means "to change into another form."[10] In two of his letters, Paul uses this same Greek word, but instead of translating the word as "transfigured," the NIV translates *metamorphoo* as "transformed": "Do not conform to the pattern of this world, but be transformed by the renewing of your mind" (Romans 12:2); "And we all, who with unveiled faces contemplate the Lord's glory, are being transformed into his image with ever-increasing glory, which comes from the Lord, who is the Spirit" (2 Corinthians 3:18).

Metamorphoo is about a complete transformation. It is where we get our English word *metamorphosis* and is likened to when the unsightly caterpillar turns into a gorgeous butterfly. Eventually, we, too, will fully transform into the doxa of God, and are transforming even now from glory to glory, doxa to doxa. Ultimately, when we receive our resurrected bodies, we will be hardly recognizable in comparison to our present glory. Jesus' transfiguration was pointing us to the future and our complete transformation in Him.

The timing of His transfiguration speaks to us about suffering and glory. He was on a death march to the cross and some say only less than a week away from fulfilling His suffering assignment.[11] None of us can really grasp the depths of agony He experienced, but as He prayed for His Father's will to be done, we read, "And being in anguish, he prayed more earnestly, and his sweat was like drops of blood falling to the ground" (Luke 22:44). Although there are many takeaways from this event, I believe the main reason He transfigured was due to the unfathomable spiritual battle He was in.

As with Stephen, whose face radiated from the fervency of persecution, genuine tribulation can draw out a visible manifestation of His glory. I mentioned briefly in chapter 2 that I had radiated from head to toe in two documented cases. What I did not explain was the difficult persecution, betrayal and false accusation that I was privately experiencing at the time. My heart had been tested fiercely by the actions of another Christian leader, but the visible glory that came upon me was the powerful assurance I needed.

When it comes to suffering and glory, we learn from Jesus our true motivation for risk taking and what we really need to endure pain. It is love. And not just ordinary love. We are talking about the love that begins with a tender and affectionate Father, a love that Jesus had known intimately and experienced already in eternity. When this same love that Jesus presents to His Bride, the Church, becomes mature in her, it looks like this poetic picture we read about in the Song of Songs:

Rivers of pain and persecution will never extinguish this flame. Endless floods will be unable to quench this raging fire that burns within you. Everything will be consumed. It will stop at nothing as you yield everything to this furious fire until it won't even seem to you like a sacrifice anymore.

8:7 TPT

It was for this love that Jesus prepared Himself to permanently remove the emotional offense between us and His Father, which was the debt of sin. The Father's love is what motivated Him to live on earth as a human being. The Father's love is what sustained Him through persecution and death on the cross. When you experience this love in your heart as He reveals it to you, you, too, will find yourself doing things you would not normally do. You will take extraordinary risks. You will endure pain, persecution, shame, even death, because His love perfectly sustains you.

The Favorite One

I was following the Facebook feed of Tricia Turnbow, co-pastor of The Worship Center in Lubbock, Texas. I had become fascinated with her intercessory journey into Israel after reading her post on April 13, 2018: "We are safe here in Tel Aviv and we are aware of the strike on Syria. We will head to the Syrian border tomorrow as planned to complete our prayer assignment there." The reason this caught my attention was that Syria was being bombed right at the time of her post by the U.S. and allied forces in response to President al-Assad's chemical attacks against his own people. In the light of this information, you would think that Tricia and her team would retreat in fear from the volatile Syrian border. Instead, she went right to the border's edge for the purposes of intercession. When I asked her about the experience, she said, "As we stood there on the border and began to intercede for the nations of Syria and Israel, explosions so loud and powerful would shake the ground beneath our feet. I began to cry out for the innocent and every person unable to escape the horrors that were happening just miles away from where I was standing. Tears streamed down my face as explosion after explosion rocked us to the core, but then I felt a shift in my heart and in the atmosphere." The shift she felt was actually His discernable response to her cry, although the outcome of her intercession for this journey is yet to be seen.

Tricia explained that this was her fourth intercessory trip to the Middle East, each trip divinely timed to intercept some very real plans of the enemy against God's beloved nation of Israel. I asked her what motivated her to do these kinds of excursions as she has now become accustomed to praying in Israel's most turbulent places and at turbulent times. "He spoke to me in a dream," she said. "His voice sounded like thunder and it shot through me like a bolt of lightning. And then, in the dream, He told me to go to Israel." This meant that she was to be ready to go to Israel and intercede whenever He called upon her to do so, an assignment that she cherishes. "I felt the weighty responsibility of this calling, and knew I had been entrusted with something very personal and precious to Him," she explained. "This made me feel like His favorite."

Tricia noticed that her spiritual authority on these assignments was greater than in other places. She said, "I remembered what you had taught about our God-given metrons of authority." The word *metron*, by the way, is a Greek word and is used to describe our apportioned faith and authority to minister within a God-assigned boundary. When we function within our metron, we see our spiritual authority produce something.[12] "Here in Israel, we saw some answers to prayer come quickly," she explained. "For example, after praying along the Gaza strip, twice the Israel Defense Forces discovered and closed underground tunnels being built by Hamas into Israel within just three days of our departure." Just to confirm her story, I had read of another prophet and intercessor sent on assignment in much the same manner as Tricia and reporting a similar outcome.[13] God was revealing the evil plans of the enemy and sending in sniper-like prophets and intercessors to shut it down.

For the prophetic intercessor, answered prayer on these levels is always an encounter with His glory. We read, "And I will do whatever you ask in my name, so that the Father may be glorified in the Son" (John 14:13). Did you know that there is an experience with His glory hidden inside of this verse just waiting to be revealed to you? When you have risked your life in intercession and then experienced the answer, there is a worship and an encounter with His presence that erupts within you. Intercession is near and dear to Jesus' heart because He forever lives to make intercession for us (see Hebrews 7:25). Tricia, a unique glory carrier, experienced the glory of answered prayer after taking some unusual risks. She risked because she had encountered His love in a dream. Echoing the apostle John, who declared himself "the disciple whom Jesus loved" (John 13:23), Tricia now calls herself "His favorite." This is not arrogance, but the fruit of one's lips after having had a heart encounter. The Bible says "there is no fear in love" (1 John 4:18), and feeling the depths of God's love removes the fear of taking on a dangerous assignment when He calls you to it. This experience with His love is the real motivation behind the risks you see being taken by such glory carriers.

Putting the Cart before the Horse

From scores of different people and places, I have heard a surplus of passionate exhortations to take risks for the name of Christ. I am sure you have, too, and we all agree that it is a right-on, very needed message. And the message is naturally infused with wonderful and extraordinary testimonies, by which we, too, are highly persuaded to share our own fiery testimonies of Jesus and to partner with the Spirit to produce jaw-dropping signs and wonders. Our zeal is piqued, our hearts are convicted, and we step out into the grisly dark world to achieve the miraculous just like our spiritual heroes. We might start out zealously for a season and see a few people saved, delivered and healed. Only our zeal becomes unsustainable when it lacks the right internal catalyst. This is where I see too many sincere and zealous people begin to cool off and retreat from the misperceived pressure to produce acts of glory in order to save the planet.

Jesus invited us to do everything He did, and much more, when He said, "Very truly I tell you, whoever believes in me will do the works I have been doing, and they will do even greater things than these, because I am going to the Father" (John 14:12). Wow! Notice that Jesus is not offended or even slighted if we do greater than He did when it comes to salvations, signs and wonders. We just have to remember what truly motivated and sustained Him. He was motivated by the tremendous exchange of love between Him and our heavenly Father. "Very truly I tell you, the Son can do nothing by himself; he can do only what he sees his Father doing, because whatever the Father does the Son also does" (5:19). This is not a statement of being enslaved, but a statement of intentional union flowing from a heart entwined with His love.

My point is this: You cannot pull love out of the air and suddenly have it. You have to experience it yourself first and then cultivate it in and through your life. What is even stranger is that we cannot force the Holy Spirit to encounter us with His love either. We have to present our hearts to Him and then wait for Him to do something about that. He will respond to you, eventually, because you are irresistible to Him. Still, we have to wait on Him to do that in His timing.

Pastor Mike Bickle, director of the International House of Prayer, made a profound statement: "It takes God to love God!" In other words, you cannot love God until He has tangibly encountered you with His love first. Then, and only then, do you have something to give back to Him and to others. You might see some miracles happen here and there because He is good to others through you, but to live and sustain this kind of zeal can only flow from an encountered heart.

Put your hand over your heart right now and say this prayer with me:

I invite You, Holy Spirit, to come and breathe upon my heart and bring my heart back to life. Encounter my heart with Your glorious intimacy. Create in me a clean heart according to Psalm 51:10. Enlarge my heart with Your supernatural love so I can "run in the path of your commandments" (Psalm 119:32). Be the architect of my heart and reshape my heart to look like You.

Glory carriers develop into courageous risk takers because they have developed into true lovers of the Holy Spirit. Because they love others deeply, they do everything with them in mind and always honor them with their actions and decisions. A glory carrier also will not go where He is not going and therefore learns how to remain connected, rather than disconnected, to His presence.

KINGDOM PRINCIPLES

1. Glory carriers do become unusual risk takers, but why they do this is often misunderstood. It is not religious fervency, but a deep love for God from the heart that motivates them.

2. The New Testament word for glory is the word *doxa*. It carries a lot of the same meaning as *kabad*, such as the notion of reputation, splendor, abundance, honor, fame, majesty and magnificence. We are going from glory to glory, doxa to doxa.

3. Jesus transfigured in glory in response to the unfathomable spiritual battle He was in right before the cross. Much like Stephen, whose face radiated from the fervency of persecution, genuine tribulation can draw out a visible manifestation of His glory.

4. Jesus knew the love of His Father intimately and for eternity. This love sustained Him while on the earth and through His death on the cross. He presents this same love to His Bride, the Church. When it matures, His love within our hearts far outweighs threats of persecution or death.

5. Pastor Mike Bickle, leader of the International House of Prayer, made a profound statement, "It takes God to love God!" In other words, you cannot love God until He has tangibly encountered you with His love first. Then, and only then, do you have something to give back to Him and to others.

THOUGHTS FOR REFLECTION

1. Have you ever encountered envy from others because of a visible manifestation of glory in your life? What was your response? Did it make you bolder or more fearful?

2. We are going from glory to glory and transforming, even now, into His image. How do you measure transformation without getting frustrated when it seems slow? (Hint: measure it over seasons or year to year.)

3. Have you ever felt pressure to perform miracles, signs and wonders as acts of achievement rather than acts flowing from a heart of love? If so, what are your thoughts now after reading this chapter?

4. Have you ever had an experience with His supernatural love? If so, how did that change you? Did you minister differently afterward?

5. A glory carrier is one because they have encountered and cultivated a relationship with the Holy Spirit. Are you a person who can follow Him without needing to understand everything? Why or why not?

I Will Not Go
without Your Presence

Evangelist Mario Murillo has a story that defies all odds.
Mario was born in San Francisco, California, a city ranked
the "least churchgoing metro in America,"[1] and one of the
last places you would expect to produce an international
evangelist. He began his preaching ministry in the drug-
obsessed, violent and occult-saturated student revolution
of Berkeley, California, and saw thousands of young students
give their lives to Christ. Then in San Jose, California, a
four-day meeting turned into a six-month crusade reaching
250,000 for Christ when the glory of God fell in an Azusa
Street–type visitation, meaning God's glory came with great
signs and wonders. Mario has continued his crusade-style
meetings in an aggressive invasion intended to reach the most
forgotten and violent youth of America. He is a glory carrier

of the heavy kind and considered a legend in California's history of revival.

As I sat down for lunch with both Mario and Mechelle Murillo at a coffee shop in Reno, Nevada, I took the opportunity to ask him about his relationship with the Holy Spirit. The demonstrations of glory throughout his life and ministry spoke clearly to me that he had a deep and mature friendship with the Spirit of God, something I wanted to know more about. Mario explained that because he did not grow up in the Church, he had no reason to doubt the authenticity of modern-day expressions of the Spirit. And when he was baptized in the Holy Spirit, he believed it to be the natural, undeniable extension of being a Christian:

"What I thought was normal, that you would be filled with power from on high and receive a heavenly language to pray in, I discovered was not normal for much of the Church at large." Mario also described the deep intimacy of relationship that he felt early on as a Christian. "This intimacy with the Spirit became a practical-living, decision-making relationship. I learned how to walk in the Spirit and be led by the Spirit," he explained. "It was truly shocking to me when I met pastors who were not led by the Spirit." He added that the great discipline of his life was to not allow those who consider being led of the Spirit to be abnormal or extracurricular to influence him away from childlike dependency on the Spirit for all his major decisions.

Mario went on to describe the pain he feels when the Holy Spirit is grieved. "God caused me to carry His presence in such a way that when I felt something interrupt it, it was agonizing to me to feel the displeasure of the Spirit." And with that, Mario's biggest concern is that people have learned to live without the glory, to function in ministry and in Christian faith without the leading of the Spirit and without the identifiable demonstration of the presence of God. "I look at men and women in ministry who are not led by the Spirit, and I wonder how they derive any sense of meaning or satisfaction? I ask, 'How does having a big church compensate for not having the presence of God? How does notoriety and celebrity make up for not knowing Him in an intimate and practical way?'" Mario said passionately, "To this day, I can't fathom that! It's the definition of misery to have the anointing lift and the presence not be there."

Every glory carrier will attest that following His presence is a daily decision, a decision that is challenged often by sophisticated arguments and a myriad of justifiable excuses. If you want to live in the unbroken fellowship of the Holy Spirit, and continue going from glory to glory, then you have to learn, really learn, how to follow Him. You have to learn connection, what it feels like and what breaks it. A certain contentment comes to your heart when you have chosen to follow His clear leading in a way that is not popular, that goes against your church's or denomination's tradition, or when it comes under the scrutiny of those in your social circle. The contentment of heart has nothing to do with being right and someone else being wrong, but all to do with having kept that intimate connection with the Spirit amid pressure while still deeply loving those who have opposed you. Glory carriers will refuse to go anywhere He is not leading them to go, adopting the impassioned heart cry of Moses: "If your Presence does not go with us, do not send us up from here" (Exodus 33:15).

The Ultimate Test

We all know that one person whose presence and influence serves to remind us about our heavenly priorities. They emulate a contagious lifestyle that puts God first, and they are not timid about reminding us to keep our ways pure. Moses was that kind of guy, a patriarch who loved God and followed Him wholeheartedly. In response to his deep friendship with God, he faithfully fathered those stubborn, rebellious Israelites and confronted them when they strayed. As I mentioned briefly in chapter 2, when Moses went up the mountain to meet with God for forty days, the Israelites temporarily lost Moses' convicting voice in their lives. We read in Exodus 32:1:

> When the people saw that Moses was so long in coming down from the mountain, they gathered around Aaron and said, "Come, make us gods who will go before us. As for this fellow Moses who brought us up out of Egypt, we don't know what has happened to him."

Instead of leading them righteously, Aaron indulged their disloyal request by making a golden calf for them to worship. The Israelites digressed back into idolatry and broke their covenant with their God, the one who delivered them from slavery in Egypt with great acts of glory.

Once Moses learned of their sin, the clash turned deadly. The Levites executed the defiant ones with the sword while God released a plague in judgement against them. Could it get any worse? Yes, it could and it did. The worst part was revealed in the Lord's next words to Moses:

> "Leave this place, you and the people you brought up out of Egypt. . . . I will send an angel before you and drive out the Canaanites, Amorites, Hittites, Perizzites, Hivites and Jebusites. Go up to the land flowing with milk and honey. But I will not go with you, because you are a stiff-necked people and I might destroy you on the way."

> 33:1–3

Essentially, He told Moses and the Israelites that He would give them the promise, but He would not give them His presence. They fully understood what that meant, especially His friend Moses. It meant they would not have His continual guidance, protection, provision or rest. Moses also knew that having God's presence among them is what set them apart from all the nations of the earth, but without Him they would be like everyone else.

The Israelites mourned in response, but Moses courageously interceded. His straightforward plea, again, was this: "If your Presence does not go with us, do not send us up from here" (v. 15). Moses was not about to go anywhere or receive anything if it cost Him the presence of His best friend. This was the ultimate test, and one we need to consider personally. The good news is, God honored his prayer and responded, "I will do the very thing you have asked, because I am pleased with you and I know you by name" (v. 17). His glorious presence continued to lead the Israelites, manifesting as a pillar of cloud by day and a fire by night.

Should we then be concerned that God could remove His manifest presence from us today? After Jesus' death and resurrection, He sent His Holy Spirit, as promised, to powerfully dwell on the inside of us and to creatively encounter us with demonstrations of His glory. You may recall that the Holy Spirit never leaves our inner man since we, as believers in Jesus, have been made His home and temple. Again, there is a difference between His Holy Spirit being in you and His Holy Spirit coming upon you, meaning that His presence and anointing could still lift off us, which is entirely different from Him leaving us altogether. Remember that He is a Person with feelings, a will, intelligence and emotions. The Bible describes how He can be grieved, quenched, extinguished and even resisted by both unbelievers and believers alike (see Ephesians 4:30; 1 Thessalonians 5:19; Acts 7:51). When this happens, the Holy Spirit does not stay where He is not honored or wanted. His presence will lift from such individuals, and He will leave in grief from their gatherings. Consequently, they do not experience His freeing, life-giving signs and wonders. They do not encounter His glory.

What we learn from God's instruction to Moses in Exodus 33 is that it is possible to live in our "Promised Land," meaning that we can live in a measure of His tangible material blessings, but without having any discernable connection to His presence. This was the deception of the lukewarm Laodicean church in Revelation. To be lukewarm is to have an attitude of the heart that is neither hot nor cold toward God, and it is an attitude that the Spirit of Christ cannot work with. Jesus addressed how this church viewed themselves as being rich and wealthy and not needing anything before He revealed their true condition: "But you do not realize that you are wretched, pitiful, poor, blind and naked" (Revelation 3:17). The deception of material comfort is that it is no substitute for the Comforter, another name for the Holy Spirit, but many neglect the Comforter because they have become materially comfortable. Eventually, this catches up to us in some form of destruction because whatever we sow to, we will eventually reap. We read, "Whoever sows to please their flesh, from the flesh will reap destruction; whoever sows to please the Spirit, from the Spirit will reap eternal life" (Galatians 6:8).

As Mario Murillo pointed out, to not have His abiding presence in your life is the most grievous way to live, but God still allows us the choice. When we choose to live and cultivate a life with the Spirit, we reap His wonderful protection, supernatural provision, wisdom, the miraculous and so much more. When we choose a life that neglects the Spirit, at best we can still live good Christian lives living according to scriptural principles, but it is a life that feels dry, disconnected and ordinary. When we are in vital union with His presence, there is the feeling of being alive and full of supernatural expectancy. There is never a dull or dry moment in His presence, and once you have tasted that life in the context of relationship with Him, you become cautious to make decisions that always include Him.

Should We Follow the Trend or Our Friend?

Like many churches that have cultivated and sustained a revival culture, there is always a supernatural history and an intense struggle behind what appears to be their current success story. My husband became the senior pastor of our church when he was only twenty-seven years old. Our church had a wealthy history with the Holy Spirit and revival, but it had lost its fire and had become, well, "churchy" and religious instead of being connected to His presence. As a young leader, Ron had considered the trendy "seeker sensitive" church model to try to revitalize our Sunday services since so many other churches were moving in that direction.

The seeker-sensitive church movement was championed by Bill Hybels, former pastor of Willow Creek Community Church just outside of Chicago, Illinois, a church that has boasted upward of twenty thousand members. The core idea behind this movement was to create Sunday services that were relevant and appealing to the "seeker," which is a term used to describe the stereotypical "unchurched Harry and Mary."[2] Armed with professional marketing research that detailed what seekers really want in a church, the traditional congregational gatherings began to transform from the stale sermons and traditional hymnal music to a more entertaining culture. The music became contemporary with flashy lights and multimedia screens, pastors began sporting tattoos and skinny jeans, sermons were shortened using illustrations from popular television and movie clips to present self-help oriented themes, and the lobbies featured coffee bars, bookstores and cozy couches.[3]

There are appealing arguments both for and against this church model, but the one thing missing was the intentional teaching and introduction of the Holy Spirit to the unchurched newcomer. The manifestation of His presence was widely thought to be offensive to the seeker, and so the Holy Spirit was put out of view like an embarrassing relative.

As this movement began to grow in popularity, the churches in our city either remained traditional or liturgical, or they adopted the seeker-friendly model, all except for us. Ron and I wanted a church that honored the Holy Spirit and we were confident we could introduce Him to unchurched newcomers, the stereotyped seekers, knowing that whatever supernatural experience took place would radically change their lives.

Do not get me wrong, I enjoyed the more modern look and feel of this movement well above the cold and stale, churchy environments of the past. And almost every contemporary-style church today has incorporated some elements of this model into its Sunday service architecture. Still, the pressure to compromise our friend, the Holy Spirit, for a seemingly successful church growth model was altogether real.

We felt a real desperation to shift and reignite the then eighty-year-old traditional Pentecostal church because it seemed to be dying out. Like many other pastors trying to survive the spiritual and cultural transition happening in our nation, we were now faced with the tough question: Should we follow the trend or follow our Friend?

Ron and I already knew what our choice would be. We chose to follow our Friend, the Holy Spirit, and in doing so we went against the grain of our entire city. That meant we dropped all ideas of following a popular church-growth model, opting for a Holy Spirit–designed model instead.

Moses insightfully shared a similar concern when faced with losing the glorious presence of the Lord: "What else will distinguish me and your people from all the other people on the face of the earth?" (Exodus 33:16).

Our choice did set us apart from everyone else and garnered the expected level of scrutiny and persecution. I say this humbly and with some humor, but eventually we did grow to become the largest Spirit-filled congregation in the city, only now with contemporary music, lights and screens, along with skinny jeans, but with respect and a high regard for the Holy Spirit. As I shared in chapter 3, the Spirit of glory has beautifully rewarded us with His amazing presence and undeniable demonstrations of His glory. The lost are radically saved, broken families are restored, bodies and minds are supernaturally healed, the demonized are set free and so much more. In addition, there is a growing felt impact upon our ultraconservative city and a growing influence in the nations.

They Did Not Follow the Spirit

One of the most troubling situations that I witnessed just after renewal came to our church involved a family who decided to transition into another fellowship. Although it hurts to have someone leave, I always try to bless those who choose to attend another church because we are all the Body of Christ. I do not believe everyone needs to go to our church or that something is wrong with them if they choose not to. In this case, however, I had a check in my spirit that something was not right about their decision. When I say that I had a check in my spirit, what I mean is that I identified a specific feeling on the inside of me that I have learned over the years to be a kind of red flag or warning from the Holy Spirit.

They had been offered a unique ministry opportunity at the other church, and on the surface, it seemed like a good decision. I did take note that the church was not a Spirit-filled congregation and asked a few more questions just to see how they felt about that. I asked, "Is the Holy Spirit in the atmosphere of a church important to you?"

The response was authentic, but not what I expected. "No, I guess not."

My spirit was vexed, but not for the reasons you might think. Deep down, of course, I want everyone to honor the Holy Spirit, which to me looks a certain way. I also realized that not everyone had been on the same journey that I had been when it came to encountering His presence, and this couple was still in a learning curve in that regard. With that said, I was not vexed over principle, but I was vexed because I knew something was not right and I could not put my finger on it. Their response about the Holy Spirit also told me that they were disconnected from Him, which meant they could not feel or sense what I was feeling.

To make a very long story short, the church became embroiled in a very public scandal. Our former congregants, due to their connection with the ministry, went through intense scrutiny over this situation and suffered much emotional distress for not only a bad decision, but a decision made so clearly disconnected from the Holy Spirit. Their story is extreme, but the takeaway is that we must always honor the Holy Spirit and remain vitally connected to Him in relationship. We simply cannot go anywhere He is not going.

Leaving Our Need to Understand

All too often our financial needs, our reasonings and our intellect interfere with our ability to fully follow where His presence is leading, especially when His leading does not make sense. Bill Johnson, senior leader of Bethel Church in Redding, California, said this: "An intellectual gospel is always in danger of creating a God that looks a lot like us— one that is our size. The quest for answers sometimes leads to a rejection of mystery. As a result, mystery is often treated as something intolerable, instead of a real treasure."[4] Just as with Tricia Turnbow's story and my story in the previous chapter, what the Holy Spirit had in mind for both of us was a complete mystery. We had to lay aside our need to understand everything if we were going to fully follow Him. Knowing and discovering Him at deeper levels, however, became the unmistakable reward.

Janelle and Nathanial, both members of our church, experienced this when the Holy Spirit began leading Janelle into some very uncomfortable and challenging decisions. Janelle shared with me that she was quite confused, but trusting, when she heard the Holy Spirit speak. He clearly told her to lay down her six-figure paying job and a promising career at an energy company to just stay home. This did not make sense at all since her husband's business income had been sporadic and they just had their first child.

The Holy Spirit then warned her to not make decisions out of fear about her finances, saying, *I'm preparing you and your husband for future ministry, but your marriage is in the balance.* This is when Janelle had to really trust Him—when His leading did not make sense. She did not know why her marriage would be in the balance. "I thought I had a great marriage!" she said. "And my husband and I both faithfully attended, served and tithed to our church." She knew His voice, however, and knew to follow where His presence was leading, even when she did not understand.

Janelle still did not doubt His leading after she left her job, and then two months later, her husband's business failed. This is when she also discovered her husband's addiction to painkillers, something that took hold that previous year following a painful shoulder surgery. They chose to pick up odd jobs between the two of them and continued to serve and give to their church despite their problems. It seemed as though they never had enough, but God had promised Janelle that He would provide as long as she trusted Him.

"Then everything went from bad to worse," Janelle said. One thing led to the other and Janelle's husband fell into heroin addiction. On the outside, it looked as if she was losing everything. On the inside, however, she was comforted. She knew the Lord had gone ahead of her and prepared her for crisis. She then gathered her pastor, mentors and friends to conduct an intervention for her husband. In response, he agreed to get help and soon entered into a Christian rehabilitation program.

"I learned to trust God in my crisis," Janelle said. "He definitely proved Himself to be faithful." The end of her story should encourage us all. By the time it was all over, Janelle and her husband ended up with a new home, a new agricultural business, a new church and a revitalized marriage. Janelle also shared how their testimony has been used powerfully in ministry. Her journey, and their subsequent victory, began when she laid down her need to understand and simply trusted and followed His presence.

What I admire most about Janelle and Nathanial's testimony is their heart to follow His presence without becoming offended. As difficult as all this was, they did not get offended at God, and they did not end up offended with each other, something much easier said than done. I felt it was important to draw this out because if there is one thing that stops people from following His presence, it is offense.

An Offended Heart Cannot Follow His Presence

All of us have experienced the sting of offense before. I would describe offense as that intense feeling of outrage that rises up inside of us when we have been insulted, emotionally injured, or have experienced injustice. Jesus taught us that offenses will come and there is no avoiding it (see Luke 17:1). In other words, we will have opportunity after opportunity to be offended, and not just offended, but highly offended. This is probably why Jesus told Peter to forgive someone "not seven times, but seventy-seven times" (Matthew 18:22). He was equipping us with the only real answer to offense. We have to set our hearts daily to forgive any offenses that come our way and to forgive well. That means we do not just forgive on a superficial level, but that we forgive from the depths of our hearts.

There was a certain sorcerer by the name of Simon that had a stronghold on the city of Samaria, having fascinated them through demonic signs and wonders. We read about him and that "everyone, from the least to the greatest, often spoke of him as 'the Great One—the Power of God.' They listened closely to him because for a long time he had astounded them with his magic" (Acts 8:10–11 NLT). When Phillip the evangelist preached the gospel in Samaria, the Holy Spirit revealed His manifest glory with even more powerful signs and wonders. Demons left people with loud shrieks, and the lame and paralyzed were healed, something that brought joy to the entire city. Surprisingly, Simon also became a believer in Jesus Christ, and he followed Phillip everywhere being "astonished by the great signs and miracles he saw" (v. 13). Simon's corrupted heart was revealed when he asked the visiting apostles, Peter and John, if he could give them money to purchase their ability to baptize people in the Holy Spirit.

Peter swiftly rebuked him for not having a heart that was right toward God, then added, "For I see that you are full of bitterness and captive to sin" (v. 23). Although we do not know exactly what sin he was captive to, we do see his heart condition. He was full of bitterness, meaning he had an offended heart. The Bible does not mention him any further, but historical figures such as Justin Martyr and other Christian apologists like Irenaeus insist he was an antichrist and continued his sorcery, even founding the heresy of Gnosticism itself.[5]

Like Simon Magus and so many others, some people stop following the presence of God because they have justified their right to be offended. They have no intention to forgive the people who have offended them, which has polluted their heart. Not only are we counseled by Jesus to forgive others if we want to be forgiven by Him, but He also points out who is blessed or not and why. He said, "Blessed are the pure in heart, for they will see God" (Matthew 5:8). We can also read this in another way. Those whose hearts are impure will not be able to see Him. Offense closes the eyes of your heart and disconnects you from His presence. You cannot see where He is going, you cannot feel where He is leading, and you end up completely out of step with Him.

Let's ask the Holy Spirit to search our hearts right now and to bring to our attention anyone we are offended with and need to forgive. As He brings people to your attention, go ahead and release them to Him by forgiving them and praying a prayer from your heart to bless them. Some situations might be more difficult than others to release, and you might need to talk to a pastor or a Christian counselor to help you heal. Still, as glory carriers we need to always do whatever it takes to remove anything standing in the way of our relationship with the Spirit of God. Even if the process is painful, we must not go anywhere without His presence.

There is a deep, refining process that takes place in the life of every glory carrier. The Holy Spirit is determined to reproduce His holy nature in you, something that can feel like a wrestling match even with the most willing vessel. As you journey deeper in relationship with Him, be prepared to encounter His glory fire. This is a purifying encounter with glory and one that calls you to deep places.

KINGDOM PRINCIPLES

1. Glory carriers will refuse to go anywhere He is not leading them to go, adopting the impassioned heart cry of Moses: "If your Presence does not go with us, do not send us up from here" (Exodus 33:15).

2. Every glory carrier will attest that following His presence is a daily decision, a decision that is challenged often by sophisticated arguments and a myriad of justifiable excuses.

3. What we learn from God's instruction to Moses in Exodus 33:1–3 is that it is possible to live in our "Promised Land," meaning that we can live in a measure of His tangible material blessings, but without having any discernable connection to His presence. This is a grievous and ultimately destructive way to live.

4. There are many trends and fads that popular ministers might assert as being the solution to grow your church. If anything forsakes the Person of the Holy Spirit, it is better to follow your Friend instead of the trend.

5. All too often, our financial needs, our reasonings and our intellect interfere with our ability to fully follow where His presence is leading, especially when His leading does not make sense. We have to lay aside our need to understand everything if we are going to fully follow Him.

THOUGHTS FOR REFLECTION

1. Just like our thriving human relationships, we have to learn connection with the Holy Spirit, what it feels like and what breaks it. What does connection with the Holy Spirit feel like to you? What, if anything, have you discovered to break that connection?

2. The Holy Spirit is a Person with feelings, a will, intelligence and emotions who can also be grieved and resisted. How do we, in the day-to-day, pay attention to not grieve or resist Him?

3. When we neglect having a relationship with the Holy Spirit, our lives begin to feel dry, disconnected and ordinary. Have you ever experienced this? If so, how did you reconnect with Him?

4. Have you ever been led by the Spirit in a way that did not make sense? What was the outcome of your experience?

5. Did you ask the Holy Spirit to bring to your attention anyone that you needed to forgive? If so, how has offense noticeably disconnected you from following His presence?

Immersed in Glory Fire

Years ago, I read *The Fire of His Holiness* by author and minister Sergio Scataglini. This amazing book challenged my thinking and convicted me so mightily that I could never read past chapter 4. My husband and I have been blessed with Sergio's ministry at our church, and we have attended a handful of his conferences as well. He carries a message of holiness unlike most people that I know. I believe the message of holiness is something you have to be called, prepared and anointed by God for. Sergio has shared both publicly and in his book that his message of holiness did emerge from a personal encounter with the Holy Spirit. Unless you are anointed by God to preach this kind of message, at best, you will sound like the stereotypical angry preacher. Sergio could speak the truth with such holy conviction, yet with tremendous love from the Father all at the same time. He also carries an unusual demonstration of glory. When the manifest presence of God fell in the room as he ministered, it felt like fire. To be more specific, it felt like holy fire.

What I learned, first from Sergio, and then in my own journey, is that personal holiness and this kind of experience of glory were very much cause and effect with a whole lot of process in between. Still, Sergio's message was difficult. He would preach often that "98 percent holiness is not enough!" He would then add, "Would you drink a glass of water that was 98 percent pure and 2 percent sewage?" Amazingly, he would say those convicting words with such love and grace that I would find myself surrendering to the fire of holiness more than I thought I ever could or would. When I did, the Holy Spirit would graciously and powerfully meet me in my decision and submerge me in His glory fire.

God's Fire-like Glory

The Holy Spirit will manifest His glory to us like fire. We read in the Bible how fire was often a symbol for the presence of God. "Now on the day that the tabernacle was raised up, the cloud covered the tabernacle, the tent of the Testimony; from evening until morning it was above the tabernacle like the appearance of fire" (Numbers 9:15 NKJV). The cloud was the glory of God, only with the quality of fire (see also 2 Chronicles 5:14; 1 Kings 8:11; Ezekiel 10:4; Exodus 40:35).

There have been many testimonies throughout history of people seeing fire on or around the buildings where anointed services were being held. Tommy Welchel, one of the last remaining persons to have physically attended the Azusa Street Revival, described meetings where there was spiritual fire seen coming up from the floor and fire coming down through the ceiling. "This is when the miracles would happen," he said.[1]

116

Kenneth Browning, a psychology student at West Virginia University, shared with me his experiences with the glory fire of God. "I was privileged to see the Lord move in signs, wonders, and glory manifestations in my church even as a young boy," he said. "For example, during a series of revival meetings, the fire department was contacted after several people in the neighborhood saw the roof of the church on fire." He further explained that the church roof was not physically on fire. It was a supernatural fire, but some in the neighborhood could see it with their physical eyes.

I, too, have a similar testimony when I ministered at a prayer conference in Chicago. One woman in attendance had invited her husband to come. Her husband was a believer in Jesus, but did not know the Holy Spirit the same way she did. That night was different, however, as he communicated to her that he was seeing flames on top of the building and did not understand why. That was also the night that we experienced a powerful angelic invasion, something you can read about in detail in my first book, *The Intercessors Handbook*.

The Bible also characterizes God in both the Old and New Testaments as a "consuming fire" (Deuteronomy 9:3; Hebrews 12:29 NASB). One scholar wrote this, "There is nothing mysterious about the Hebrew and Greek words translated 'consuming fire.' They mean exactly that—a fire that utterly consumes or destroys."[2] He is a consuming fire, the Bible says, because He is a jealous God and will not share His glory with worthless idols. He is perfectly jealous for our hearts in this regard because our hearts rightfully belong to Him (see Deuteronomy 4:23–24; Isaiah 42:8). When you awaken to how passionate He is for you, that He is fiercely jealous for you, and He truly believes You should be fully His, it does something to your heart. It calls your attention and invites you to walk toward the fire rather than away from it. When

His glory fire comes, it comes to consume whatever stands in the way of your wholehearted devotion toward Him. It comes to devour anything that is in the way of His glorious purposes toward you.

Touched by His Fire

I was ministering at a tent revival in Merced, California. The name Merced means "mercy" in Spanish, something I felt was particularly significant for this event. The crowd, mostly gang members and their families, desperately needed to experience the mercy and glory of God. As soon as I arrived, I received a text from a prophet in Oregon who had no knowledge of where I was ministering. He wrote, *I heard an audible voice last night. It said, "Jennifer will be shot at, but it will be okay."*

For some reason, I did not discern his words as being the end of the story, but more like a warning. I grew up about thirty minutes from this city and in a very similar environment. I was not afraid, but I knew it could get out of control quickly unless God protected me. I had a small army of intercessors attending with me who prayed into the matter. After I spoke and ministered to the hardened, but desperate crowd, a very rough-looking man approached me at the end of the service.

"I came here today believing I was unreachable, and I had no plan to change," he said, fighting back tears. "But you got through to me and then God got to me." This man had served several prison terms and looked as hard as a rock, that is, until that moment. Although he did not see with his physical eyes the spiritual flames that had descended into the atmosphere of the tent, I could feel God's glory and discern what was taking place, and his calloused heart was undeniably impacted. That night he gave his life to Jesus, having been confronted by the all-consuming fire of God. His hard heart had been penetrated by the fire of His glory and then turned toward His holy purposes.

You might be asking the question then, Was that a false prophecy? Looking back, I can definitely see the intense spiritual warfare happening for this man's heart. Either way, I did not hear those prophetic words as being something that would happen. I heard it as something that could happen and that we needed to build a hedge in prayer and pray through it. Thankfully, I was not shot at, and I ministered to this rough crowd uninterrupted.

God's glory fire can also fall from heaven to either consume or ignite something or someone. His fire fell from heaven upon some of the sacrifices in the Old Testament, burning them completely up (see 1 Chronicles 21:26; 2 Chronicles 7:1; 1 Kings 18:38). Prophesying about Jesus, John the Baptist said, "I baptize you with water for repentance. But after me comes one who is more powerful than I. . . . He will baptize you with the Holy Spirit and fire" (Matthew 3:11). The word *baptized* in this passage is the Greek word *baptízō*, which means to be immersed and submerged.[3] After Jesus' ascension, the Holy Spirit fell upon the one hundred twenty believers in the Upper Room (see Acts 1:13–15) as "cloven tongues like as of fire" (2:3 KJV), igniting the early Church. Being baptized with fire, then, means to be fully immersed in, saturated with and consumed by His fire.

For some, a physical sensation of fire is how they identify the presence of the Holy Spirit. Andrea Hinojos, photographer, wife and mother of four, shares her experience with glory fire. "Often when I worship spontaneously to the Lord, I will feel His fire on my back," she explained. "I also feel it in different ways. For example, when I respond for special prayer at church or at a conference, I will feel a heavier, weightier fire from the top of my head to my feet." Andrea's supernatural connection with the Holy Spirit can really be seen when she prays for people one-on-one. His manifest presence comes upon them as she prays, and He encounters them with signs and wonders. I think the word picture is clear that when the fire of His glory falls upon you, He is making a point with your life. Your life has been made a sacrifice unto Him, and you are to live from that moment on ignited as a carrier of glory fire.

I have also learned from experience that when God touches you with the fire of His glory, a purifying fire, something shifts within you. I was ministering in Memphis, Tennessee, at a conference for women in leadership and ministry. As we enthusiastically praised and worshiped together, the tangible glory of God fell upon the room first in a deep, supernaturally created worship. This kind of worship is a worship from the Spirit. It feels elevated and heavenly and seems to gather the entire room into a felt unity. It is a worship that flows in its quality like a river from another realm, even though these were songs that were familiar to us. Next, the glory of God stood before us like a wall of fire. I could feel the heat in front of me and sense and see with my spiritual eyes the shape of this flaming wall.

I noticed immediately the increase in accuracy as I prophesied to people. For instance, by the unction of the Spirit I had a vision about a woman in attendance and described to her what I saw: "I see curriculum on a shelf! You need to finish the curriculum! You are going to the nations with the curriculum!" She screamed and then fell onto the floor. She described later of her many attempts to create teaching curriculum, but not really knowing why. They were half done and just sitting on her shelves. She had been praying about it and had considered letting that desire go. The Holy Spirit had something else in mind.

After experiencing the glory fire in this setting, I could see spiritually with much better clarity as if the eyes of my heart had been purified even further. Afterward, however, I was concerned that I could lose that clarity and began to seek Him in prayer to search my heart. This is the challenging aftermath that often accompanies encounters with glory fire because it has a convicting quality to it. You touch something deeper in Him and then feel as if you cannot live without it. It is something that pulls you into His purifying process.

Holy Tension

When I was out running errands one day, I recognized someone who had come to our church off and on in the past. He asked me some positive questions about the church, then loudly asked me, "If you are saved, then you are always saved, right?" He was indirectly referring to the doctrine of *eternal security* without using the actual term. Eternal security is the belief that once we have become born again, then we can never ever lose our salvation under any circumstance.[4] I like this guy, but I saw the setup because he lives his life according to his own righteousness. He is probably not a Noah, David, or even a Lot, but he lives out something I call "relative righteousness."

That would be a form of self-righteousness that is not based on a real relationship with Jesus, but a righteousness based in comparison. The thought behind it is, *I don't murder anyone, I don't hate anyone, I don't steal, so I'm okay.* This is also where many people mistakenly think they will go to heaven without ever having surrendered to Jesus as their personal Lord and Savior. They hold fast to the belief that they will go to heaven when they die because they are comparatively good people. As for the man I was talking to, I actually do believe he has a relationship with Jesus, just an immature one, and he is definitely disconnected from the Holy Spirit. He has yet to encounter His glory fire.

Now I am sure both you and I take comfort knowing we have been made right with our heavenly Father because of Jesus' sacrifice on the cross. We do not have to fear that we will lose our eternal home in heaven because we have had a bad season. So then why would personal holiness matter at all? I know the answer is obvious, but we have to bring this thought back into the context of relationship. Friendship with the Holy Spirit is synonymous with friendship with the holy. Holy is who He is, and as glory carriers, we will come into tension with His holy nature. I liken this to a very real wrestling match with a good God who deeply loves you, but whose very presence demands a transformation from you. These are often deeply internal and painful transformations that we would prefer to rebuff, ignore, challenge or argue with. If you do not transform, you will remain in a frustrating tension with Him. You will not have the internal capacity to handle His glory fire as it will overwhelm you.

The prophet Isaiah, for example, described his overwhelming vision of the Lord and angels calling out the praises of God to one another. He wrote, "At the sound of their voices the doorposts and thresholds shook and the temple was filled with smoke" (6:4). The smoke, in this passage, was actually the cloud of glory. You would think Isaiah would be overcome with a holy ecstasy in this atmosphere of glory and worship, but instead the prophet had a personal meltdown. He shouted, "Woe to me! . . . I am ruined! For I am a man of unclean lips, and I live among a people of unclean lips, and my eyes have seen the King, the LORD Almighty" (v. 5). Apparently, this trash-talking prophet had an encounter with the glory that surfaced his potty mouth with overwhelming conviction. Relief did not come until the seraphim burnt his mouth with a fiery coal from the altar, something that reinforces the concept that glory carriers must be purified, continuously, with His fire (see vv. 6–7).

How to Continuously Carry Glory Fire

I say this humorously, but writing this chapter finally inspired some maturity in me to go ahead and push further ahead into Sergio's book, but now with a more confident heart. It has been several years since I laid it down, and I laughed so hard looking now through its contents. It is obvious I had read his book through the lens of self-condemnation. I hope that encourages you. You see, the way we measure growth and transformation is not from day-to-day, but over the periods of years and seasons. Sergio wrote this, "If you want to receive His holy fire, you have to be willing to be transformed."[5] Transformation is ongoing. It is not a one-time encounter and immersion in the fire of His glory, but many encounters. With that said, here are a few points to help you carry His glory fire:

1. You will always be uncomfortable.

Glory carriers should always have the sense of being continuously stretched and challenged from the inside out. We are moving from glory to glory, meaning we are always changing and transforming, which is uncomfortable. This is an occasion to lean into the Holy Spirit, however, who is our "Comforter" (John 14:26 KJV).

2. Understand the purpose of tension.

A catapult is an ancient weapon of warfare designed to launch projectiles at great distances. What makes a catapult effective is that it works through tension. It is the tension that creates the force to launch a weapon effectively. Tension with the Holy Spirit can feel like a wrestling match, but this is what shapes you and sharpens you to be the arsenal of fire that He is making you into.

3. Remind yourself, daily, that you are not condemned.

Remember that self-condemnation disconnects you from the Holy Spirit and then throws you down the black hole of emotional turmoil. Empty your heart daily of condemning thoughts, feelings and mistakes already repented of. A glory carrier must stay connected to the Holy Spirit.

4. Do not quit when you fail.

Everyone fails and many glory carriers, historically, have failed notoriously and still got up to carry the fire again. It is how you fail that counts. A glory carrier learns to own and repent of their mistakes, live in His mercy, and never give their confidence away (see Hebrews 10:35).

5. Keep the fire hot.

A glory carrier learns how to stay on fire and keep the fire hot. We are reminded through Paul's instruction to Timothy to stay stirred up and to fan the flames of glory (see 2 Timothy 1:6). Big conferences and gatherings are helpful, but we have to solve this in the day-to-day routine of our lives. Keeping ourselves in the fire of His glory daily looks different from person-to-person, but going spiritually dormant is not an option we can accept for ourselves.

We are made to carry His glory fire, and we were made for holiness, only we cannot do either on our own. Instead, it is the outflow of an intimate heart relationship with the Holy Spirit, the Source of all holiness, as we share our lives with Him. The Spirit of Christ loves us wholeheartedly. As much as the Father loves Jesus and Jesus loves the Holy Spirit, is as much as the Holy Spirit loves you and me. Many times, I can barely grasp the thought that the Holy Spirit perfectly champions us and never fails to intercede for us. He responds to us in relationship, but He is perfectly holy. This is where the tension resides. He is a beautiful encounter from beginning to end, but His nature will challenge and afflict ours until we have been transformed into the very nature of Jesus Christ.

What are you feeling right now? It is normal to feel very challenged with these concepts. My prayer is that you accept the challenge, and yet be perfectly hopeful and excited to experience the Spirit of glory on levels you never thought possible. Nearness with Him brings us into His world and into unusual encounters with His glory.

KINGDOM PRINCIPLES

1. The Holy Spirit will manifest His glory to us like fire. We read in the Bible how fire was often a symbol for the presence of God and can also represent His jealous nature toward us. When His glory fire comes, it comes to consume whatever stands in the way of your wholehearted devotion toward Him.

2. Prophesying about Jesus, John the Baptist said, "I baptize you with water for repentance. But after me comes

one who is more powerful than I. . . . He will baptize you with the Holy Spirit and fire" (Matthew 3:11). The word *baptized* in this passage is the Greek word *baptizō*, which means to be immersed and submerged. Being baptized with fire, then, means to be fully immersed, saturated and consumed with His fire.

3. Jesus has perfectly and without fail restored us to Himself and His Father through faith in His name. We have been restored to glory (see Romans 8:30). We can carry His glory once again, but the process is where we come into relational tension with the Holy Spirit who wants nothing more than nearness with us.

4. Friendship with the Holy Spirit is synonymous with friendship with the holy. Holy is who He is and as glory carriers, we will come into tension with His holy nature.

5. When the fire of His glory falls upon you, He is making a point with your life. Your life has been made a sacrifice unto Him, and you are to live from that moment ignited as a carrier of glory fire.

THOUGHTS FOR REFLECTION

1. Have you ever encountered His glory in a way that felt like fire? What did that feel like? What impact did that have on you afterward?

2. Do you struggle with self-condemnation? If so, how do you reconcile a growing lifestyle of holiness, the trademark of a true glory carrier, with your inevitable failures and shortcomings?

3. Has God-inspired transformation ever felt like a wrestling match between you and the Holy Spirit? If so, how?

4. How do you measure holiness in your life? By comparison to those around you, or by what is written in the Bible?

5. As a glory carrier, how do you stay on fire and keep the fire of His glory hot in your life? How do you overcome spiritual dormancy in the day-to-day routine of your life?

Encounters
with the Glory World

When Jesus and His mother and disciples were at a wedding in Cana of Galilee, the hosts of the wedding had run out of wine. We read in John 2 how Jesus' mother turned to Him and said, "They have no more wine" (v. 3). By the way, this was not a statement of need but a veiled request. Jesus offered a slight protest over the timing of what she suggested, "Woman, why do you involve me? . . . My hour has not yet come" (v. 4). Reading between the lines of their comments, you get the feeling He might have done this miracle before, only privately. Jesus told the servants to fill with water the available six pots that were normally used for Jewish ceremonial washing and cleansing. They did so, then Jesus instructed them to draw some of the water out and take it to the master of the banquet. When they did this, they discovered the water had turned into a high-quality wine, and now they were well supplied with at least one hundred twenty gallons' worth (see vv. 5–11). Wow! Jesus' first public miracle revealed His glory and, because it met a need, did not offend the wedding party.

Has this miracle ever occurred since then? Not that I have heard of or could verify after researching the possibility. My question for both you and for me, and I point this out somewhat humorously, is: What would happen if the Holy Spirit did it again? What if He did this same miracle in our modern American context? Many American Christians believe alcohol is wrong and for good reasons, and a miracle of glory that turns water into wine would most likely come under condemnation and be put down in much of the Christian media. The nature of miracles, however, is to reveal God's glory, not our cultural preferences. We have to grasp this, or we might become offended with new and unusual manifestations of glory, in whatever manner He chooses to reveal Himself, and call evil what God intended to be good.

Compelling Demonstrations of Glory

A glory carrier develops into a compelling demonstration of the Holy Spirit's many manifestations of glory. These captivating manifestations are the visible broadcast of His goodness. They are like a persuasive invitation for relationship by all those who see and experience it. Such manifestations can include miraculous healings, words of knowledge, deliverance from demons and much more. We can never limit what the Holy Spirit wants to do. We have to remain open and unoffended at the Holy Spirit when He does something outside of our grid of understanding. He is infinite in His expression, and going from glory to glory means He will by His very nature manifest a new thing in our midst (see Isaiah 43:19).

Holy Laughter

One of the most offensive manifestations of the Spirit of glory is a phenomenon described as holy laughter, in which people begin to laugh hysterically as if they were drunk, but for no apparent reason.

Prior to ever hearing about this kind of manifestation of glory, I experienced it for the first time in the early 1990s at the end of a church service. An altar worker prayed for me, and I just laughed and laughed and could not stop for close to twenty minutes. I have witnessed this manifestation many times and in many places, including my own church. I welcome this encounter in my life as it seems to cleanse me of deep sadness, which reflects the proverb, "A merry heart doeth good like a medicine" (Proverbs 17:22 KJV). I can see the controversy, though, because holy laughter appears very disorderly and as having no overt purpose.

Testimonies of uncontrollable laughter have been observed since the 1800s, most notably in the Wesleyan meetings,[1] only John Wesley viewed the phenomenon as being of the devil.[2] It seemed to find some acceptance in the 1980s, however, during the signs and wonders meetings with John Wimber, leader of the Vineyard Movement, and then in the 1990s with South African evangelist Rodney Howard-Browne.[3]

Sid Roth, host of the popular Christian television show *It's Supernatural!*, wrote about his experience with holy laughter in his blog.

> We had a "repentance" meeting and were all serious. We asked God to convict us and bring a spirit of weeping upon us. We waited for a while—nothing happened. After about

15 minutes someone began to giggle. We tried to stifle our mouths because we were there to weep. After another few minutes someone else started to giggle. We could contain it no more—we hit the floor and laughed uproariously for about 3 hours. We had been under condemnation for years because of religious spirits. We didn't need to be weeping right then—we were getting delivered and getting to know "Abba" (daddy).[4]

Author, entrepreneur and minister Tonya Dennis from Atlanta, Georgia, shares her experience with holy laughter after an apostle prayed and laid hands on her to receive. She said, "Each time it felt like God was delivering me from something, or I was laughing over my enemies, or I was receiving a new measure of joy from the Lord for my journey. I am reminded of the Scripture Proverbs 31:25: 'She can laugh at the days to come.'" I would say her testimony is a good summary of what occurs with those struck by supernatural joy from the Holy Spirit.

Angel Feathers

The Bible tells us that there are angels all around us. We read this powerful promise: "The angel of the LORD encamps around those who fear him, and he delivers them" (Psalm 34:7). If you fear the Lord, then His angel comes to stay with you. The Bible also says, "Are not all angels ministering spirits sent to serve those who will inherit salvation?" (Hebrews 1:14). This means that if you are a believer in Christ, you have angels personally assigned to help you. Even if we cannot see the angels with our physical eyes, they are still with us. Regardless, glory carriers often do see, hear, or feel the presence of these angels. Angels exist in this realm, and as we press into the Spirit of glory, we will encounter His angels as well. Or, we might just encounter their feathers. I will explain what I mean.

I was sitting alongside some ministers at a conference in Las Vegas while guest speaker Shawn Bolz began ministering in the Holy Spirit's gift of the word of knowledge. The accuracy and nature of this ministry encouraged people that God knew them specifically and personally. As he ministered, I looked down on the floor, and by my feet was a cluster of small white feathers, maybe around ten to twelve of them, all less than half of an inch long. I pointed them out to the people sitting by because I knew Shawn would be ministering in our vicinity soon. How did I know that? I could tell by the location of the feathers that angels were nearby, and I discerned they were most likely directing the flow of ministry toward us. Within moments, Shawn began ministering to a married couple sitting right behind us through the word of knowledge and the gift of prophecy.

International minister Joshua Mills shared a story about a backslidden girl who lived in the Arctic.[5] He said that one of her parents was a pastor who had given the girl one of Joshua's books about the glory realm and the accompanying signs and wonders. She kept the book, but did not read it until the day she stayed home from work with an illness. As she read the testimonies of feathers manifesting in some of his meetings, an actual feather fell out of the air in front of her. She dismissed it as being a coincidence and tried to explain it away in her mind. As she kept reading, however, another feather fell in front of her which got her attention. Finally, as she was reading the testimonies, another miracle occurred. A burst of gold-colored sparkles and dust miraculously came out of her wall. This is another manifestation of glory that I will discuss in the next section. Either way, she became overwhelmed in the presence of the Holy Spirit's glory and got on her knees and gave her life back to Jesus. Not only that, but soon after her husband did the same, having turned his life from being a drug lord to Jesus Christ.

Testimonies of feathers appearing out of nowhere have become more common these days, especially by those seeking relationship with the Holy Spirit who then tap into the glory world. Sometimes you will notice a small feather float down in front of you as you pray or worship. Other times, feathers will appear in a much more dramatic fashion. As much as I enjoy the manifestation of angel feathers as a sign of His glory, I am not so much looking for the feathers; I am looking for Him. Still, it tells me what is going on and is a sure sign from the glory realm. Angels are near, they are on Kingdom assignment, and they have come to help us.

Gold Dust and Oil

The late Ruth Ward Heflin, an amazing glory carrier and revivalist, was a student and forerunner of the Holy Spirit's creative manifestations of glory. Often quoted as saying that the glory is "the realm of eternity,"[6] she was not afraid of the new thing that God might do. Likewise, her revival campground in Ashland, Virginia, seemed to host a lot of "firsts." For instance, many people and churches today experience a supernatural phenomenon involving gold dust and oil. Typically, gold flakes mysteriously appear on the body of a person, oil begins to flow from that person's body or hands, or both happen at the same time. I am not sure if this was a brand-new manifestation of His glory, but there was a first time for this in our generation. Here is the testimony of how this was introduced.

Brazilian minister Silvania Machado shared how she was miraculously healed of a degenerative bone disease. She had been invited to an evangelical church in her native country and the pastor prayed for her and encouraged her to believe in Jesus and to trust Him to be her Healer. Five days later, she did believe in Jesus and was miraculously healed from a lifetime of suffering. Silvania and her husband had been invited to a prayer vigil in the Brazilian jungle with over a hundred people in attendance. She had received a prophetic word that she would flow in the Spirit's ministry of healing and began asking the Lord for a sign. When she asked for a sign, the miracle of oil appeared, and she became covered in oil from head to toe. At another one of these prayer vigils, she again asked for a sign. This time the Lord poured out gold dust upon her. She was completely covered with gold for nearly six weeks, so distinctly so that when she bathed, gold recovered her almost immediately.[7]

Silvania's testimony was recorded on video and shown to Ruth Heflin in 1998 by the American minister who had prayed in Brazil for Silvania to receive the Holy Spirit. A few weeks after they viewed this video, then showed it to attendees at the campground, a similar manifestation began to appear. One woman, a camp meeting attendee, found a gold nugget on the floor after it mysteriously dropped from her clothing while using the restroom. Others began to have gold dust appear on their hair and clothing during the services, and in nonreligious settings as well. Later, when Ruth Heflin ministered at a Baptist church in Atlanta, Georgia, the pastor was reported as having oil, at least half a cup's worth, flow right from his hands.[8]

I have experienced this miracle as well, most noticeably after I had ministered at a Christian business meeting at Living Streams Church in Bangkok, Thailand. I remember having just thirty minutes to speak, but that was enough for the Holy Spirit to release His glory upon the attendees. After I had returned to my hotel, I noticed my hands were covered with gold dust and oil. I was so overcome by that.

Just as with the supernatural appearance of angel feathers, there are many testimonies of people who have experienced the Holy Spirit's glory through gold dust and oil in various settings. With that said, Silvania's miracle was supposedly debunked through a scientific investigation conducted by *Charisma* magazine in 1999 that concluded her glitter and oil were fake. I tried to locate the actual article myself as so many heresy hunters quoted it, but I could not find it. Was Silvania's gold and oil a false miracle? Only God knows the truth, but amazingly the Holy Spirit's manifestation of gold dust and oil still continues today in the lives of ordinary people as well as those of reputation.

Supernatural Weight Loss

One of the strangest miracles of glory that I have ever come across is the miracle of supernatural weight loss. It seems almost too good to be true, but we cannot be offended at the new things He chooses to do. Supernatural weight loss is an incredible manifestation of His presence that displays His extreme goodness. As I began to write into this, I did not know of anyone personally who has had this miracle happen having only read about it and seen the miracle on a YouTube video. I decided then to ask my Facebook friends if they had experienced this miracle before. Many came forward with their testimonies. Here are a few:

One minister, Richard Stutzman, posted a video of a sweet-natured woman from Mexico who gave her testimony through her English-speaking husband about receiving supernatural weight loss after Richard prayed for her.[9] Before a conference session, she heard the clear and gentle voice of the Spirit. He asked her, "What would you like for yourself?" She humbly replied, "Nothing. I am okay." But during the service, Richard was impressed by the Holy Spirit to ask her a delicate question. He asked, "Would you like me to pray for you to lose weight?" If they were to be honest, most women would be offended at even the mere suggestion, but this did not take place with her. She gladly received prayer for supernatural weight loss and began to feel a loosening almost immediately. By the next morning, and to the amazement of her somewhat skeptical husband, she had lost seven inches off her waist. Even her feet became smaller, making her unable to wear her shoes, which were all too big. It appears that the inconvenience of this miracle is needing a new wardrobe in the end.

Donna Grisham, coordinating producer for *Sid Roth's It's Supernatural!* television show, experienced supernatural weight loss when international minister David Herzog was a guest on the show. Donna described her experience: "When David called out, 'Supernatural weight loss is taking place!,' I said out loud, 'That's mine, in Jesus' name!'"[10] Donna had tried on a pair of pants earlier in the week but could not wear them because they were too tight. After this miracle, however, she put them on the next day with ease. She added, "What was so neat was the weight kept coming off!"[11] Her weight loss was so impactful that Sid Roth had Donna share her testimony on one of his radio shows.

Again, as I was reviewing the testimonies that came through on my Facebook and reviewed their desperate stories of struggle with weight loss, the Holy Spirit moved upon me to lay hold of this specific manifestation of His glory. I gave less than a day's notice to my online community and announced a FB Live teaching and prayer for supernatural weight loss for anyone who wanted to join in. It was one of the most spontaneous things I have ever done.

The Holy Spirit's goodness was shocking as I taught God's word about asking and receiving from Him and that He is the God who does the impossible. Then I prayed for all who needed healing in their bodies from issues that caused weight gain such as hormonal imbalances, thyroid disorders and pancreas problems. Next, I worked the attendees through their emotional triggers and traumas with food such as comfort eating, food abuse, bitterness that leads to weight gain (see Numbers 5:27) and using excess weight to protect themselves from sexual predators (this is more common than people realize). Finally, I prayed for the miracle of weight loss.

Immediately, the interactive thread filled up with comments like, *I feel electricity. I feel heat and cold on my body. I am shaking right now. I am crying uncontrollably!* The testimonies began rolling in by the next morning. There were a handful of people who lost five pounds overnight, one woman lost three inches on her waist overnight, two women showed before pictures of their very tight pants and then an after picture with the same pants now hanging loosely on their bodies, and then several who suffered chronic fatigue got their energy back and started running, walking and dancing when they could not do that before. It was powerful and glorious, and yet so simple and effortless at the same time. When you move in the glory, you flow with His river without striving. He does all the work.

Manna

Another unusual and powerful manifestation of God's glory is the supernatural appearance of manna. We probably all know what manna is—the bread of heaven that was miraculously supplied each morning to the Israelites when they wandered through the desert for forty years (see Exodus

16; Psalm 78:24). The Bible describes manna as white in color and tasting like wafers made with honey, and we can assume it must have had some healing qualities to it since the Israelites never got weak or sick as they journeyed (see Exodus 16:31; Numbers 11:7; Psalm 105:37). The provision of manna ceased when the Israelites entered the Promised Land under the leadership of Joshua, but it seems to have made a reappearance in our day.

Drs. Harold and Kaye Beyer, both Lutherans, had experienced for over four decades the miraculous appearing of manna in either Harold's hands or in his Bible always in the same place at Revelation 2:17: "Whoever has ears, let them hear what the Spirit says to the churches. To the one who is victorious, I will give some of the hidden manna." On one occasion, the Holy Spirit spoke to Harold to put four empty pill bottles in his bag although he did not know why. When he had a sudden heart attack and was in the hospital, those pill bottles were miraculously filled with manna, which he ate like medicine. What was expected to be a month's stay for recovery in the hospital ended up being only a week, a recovery attributed to healing through the provision of supernatural manna.[12]

Dr. Theresa Phillips, founder of Global Prophetic Voice in St. Charles, Illinois, has also received manna on several occasions. She described how it appears neatly stacked up or scattered on the floor. Once she found manna on her lap, and another time she found it in her Bible. She said, "We never really look for this miracle to happen, but when it does I always see an angel present." She explained that it tastes like a cracker, sometimes salty, at other times oily like a potato chip and other times sweet. "We make sure to give the manna to those who are sick in our meetings," she added. "If there is enough, we freely distribute it to everyone."

The Earth Will Know His Glory

The prophet Habakkuk saw well into the future and prophesied into this generation. He said, "For the earth will be filled with the knowledge of the glory of the LORD as the waters cover the sea" (2:14). Think deeply about what the Spirit wrote through him for us to consider today. The entire earth will know His glory because you and I, ordinary people, have simply fallen in love with the Person of the Holy Spirit, and His glory has come to rest miraculously upon our lives.

I asked a private group of moms, dads and singles who cherish the Holy Spirit to share with me their unusual experiences with His glory. Keep in mind that these are normal, everyday people of no ministry reputation and their stories are outstanding. They cited several miraculous appearances of beautiful gemstones, pearls and gold nuggets while they worshiped Jesus at their church or in their personal prayer times. Others claimed the appearance of glory dust and oil on their physical bodies, usually in the context of worship. A few persons who needed dental work received it miraculously, and their ailing teeth were supernaturally filled with solid gold. Some described the appearances of angels, while others spoke of oil and water dripping from the church ceilings or right out of the air. Almost all of them said they have seen the angel feathers in various settings and in a variety of different colors.

With the instruction to not be offended at the new thing He might do, perhaps you are concerned about becoming deceived at false miracles. Your concern is valid, and the Bible does warn us to "test the spirits" (1 John 4:1) and to "test all things" (1 Thessalonians 5:20–21 NKJV). Here are a few foolproof tests to help you do that:

1. Does the miracle point people to Jesus?

The Lord spoke clearly through the prophet Isaiah: "I will not give my glory to anyone else" (Isaiah 42:8 NLT). True glory carriers love the Holy Spirit too much to turn the attention gained by the miracle to themselves. They are intentional to honor the Source, the Holy Spirit, and turn the hearts and gaze of people to Jesus Christ.

2. Do they use the miracle to solicit money?

Glory carriers are conscientious to preserve the authenticity of the miracles that emerge from their relationship with the Spirit of God. Even if they are full-time ministers and rely on financial support to live, they will still have integrity in the way they present their financial needs. They will not prostitute the manifestations of His glory or use slimy communication tactics to solicit money from you.

3. Is the miracle biblical? Does it reflect the heart of our heavenly Father?

There are many miracles of glory happening today that are already written clearly about in the Bible, while others seem to be written about only conceptually. Still, I always look for that "go-to" verse for every manifestation of His glory because I believe there will be one. For example, the appearance of angel feathers is more conceptual, but many psalms reference dwelling in the "shadow" of His wings (see Psalms 17:8; 36:7; 57:1). Even the manifestation of supernatural weight loss is found conceptually in the Bible, reflecting His extreme goodness. He gives us a new "garment of praise for the spirit of heaviness" (Isaiah 61:3), and His yoke is easy and His burden light (see Matthew 11:30). For some, losing weight supernaturally is more about being physically healed than anything else. He is our Healer and that would include being healed of an unhealthy weight.

As a glory carrier, you are being invited to encounter the glory world perhaps in ways you never considered or even thought possible. Going from glory to glory means there will always be something new that He will do. Speaking for myself, I want to be the first in line for anything new He is doing in the earth. My heart cry to the Spirit of glory is, *More, Lord! Give me much more of You!*

Let's refuse to be skeptical. Let's refuse to be offended at the unusual. Our greatest adventures of glory are just on the horizon, and He is asking us, *Will the new begin with you?*

KINGDOM PRINCIPLES

1. We have to remain open and unoffended at the Holy Spirit when He does something outside of our grid of understanding. He is infinite in His expression and going from glory to glory means He will by His very nature manifest a new thing in our midst (see Isaiah 43:19).

2. The prophet Habakkuk saw well into the future and prophesied into this generation. He said, "For the earth will be filled with the knowledge of the glory of the LORD as the waters cover the sea" (2:14).

3. The entire earth will know His glory because you and I, ordinary people, have simply fallen in love with the Person of the Holy Spirit, and His glory has come to rest miraculously upon our lives.

4. With the instruction to not be offended at the new thing He might do, we are still admonished to "test the spir-

its" (1 John 4:1) and to "test all things" (1 Thessalonians 5:20–21 NKJV).

5. We test the validity of miracles by asking these questions: Does the miracle point people to Jesus? Do they prostitute the miracle to solicit money? Is the miracle biblical? Does it reflect the heart of our heavenly Father?

THOUGHTS FOR REFLECTION

1. You are being invited to encounter the glory world in ways you never thought possible. Does this excite you or make you apprehensive? Explain.

2. Have you ever experienced holy laughter, the appearance of angel feathers or the miracle of gold dust and/ or oil?

3. What are your thoughts about the even stranger manifestations of His glory such as encounters with angels, supernatural weight loss or the appearance of manna?

4. Have you ever heard about or read about a miracle that really offended you? Why did it offend you? Did it hold up to the test questions presented in this chapter?

5. Going from glory to glory means there will always be something new that He will do. How excited are you to experience the new?

Appendix

Receiving Your Spiritual Language through Holy Spirit Baptism

My understanding as a teenager was to "seek" the Holy Spirit and then the Holy Spirit would take over my mouth. At a youth camp, a pastor excitedly told me that the Holy Spirit was there and encouraged me to speak out. I did exactly that and I received.

Edwin Smith

Glory carriers demonstrate the manifest presence of God with signs and wonders because they have cultivated over time an intimate friendship with the Spirit of God. Every friendship has a starting point, however, and I believe friendship with the Holy Spirit begins with the baptism in the Holy Spirit. We read in the Bible how this experience is necessary for us to walk in the power of the Spirit.

Holy Spirit Baptism in the Bible

Let's look at two biblical promises: First, John the Baptist said, "I baptize you with water for repentance. But after me comes one who is more powerful than I, whose sandals I am not worthy to carry. He will baptize you with the Holy Spirit and fire" (Matthew 3:11). Later, Jesus said, "For John baptized with water, but in a few days you will be baptized with the Holy Spirit. . . . You shall receive power when the Holy Spirit comes on you" (Acts 1:5, 8).

The Bible illustrates clearly that when you are baptized in the Holy Spirit, He gifts you with a supernatural language. This is the sure sign that you have received the promise of the Spirit. Let's look at this in Scripture:

> When the day of Pentecost came, they were all together in one place. Suddenly a sound like the blowing of a violent wind came from heaven and filled the whole house where they were sitting. They saw what seemed to be tongues of fire that separated and came to rest on each of them. All of them were filled with the Holy Spirit and began to speak in other tongues as the Spirit enabled them. (Acts 2:1–4)

> While Peter was still speaking these words, the Holy Spirit came on all who heard the message. The circumcised believers who had come with Peter were astonished that the gift of the Holy Spirit had been poured out even on Gentiles. For they heard them speaking in tongues and praising God. (10:44–46)

A third verse in Acts illustrates a direct connection between tongues and Spirit baptism: "When Paul placed his hands on them, the Holy Spirit came on them, and they spoke in tongues and prophesied" (9:6).

Other passages in the New Testament reveal the same truth, only indirectly. For example, in Acts 8, the apostles in

146

Jerusalem had heard that there were disciples being made in Samaria. Keep in mind that these were new believers in Jesus who had only been water baptized. The apostles traveled to Samaria and prayed for the new believers to receive the Holy Spirit "because the Holy Spirit had not yet come on any of them; they had simply been baptized in the name of the Lord Jesus. Then Peter and John placed their hands on them, and they received the Holy Spirit" (vv. 16–17). There had to have been some kind of evidence or sign to prove that they had received. The biblical account does not say directly that the new believers spoke in tongues, but something took place that was so obvious that Simon Maga offered the apostles money to give him the ability to lay hands on people to receive the Holy Spirit, too. Simon's offer was met with a swift and stern rebuke by the apostle Peter, who said, "May your money perish with you, because you thought you could buy the gift of God with money!" (v. 8:20).

The apostle Paul powerfully converted to Christianity, having been confronted by Jesus Himself on the road to Damascus. What is interesting is he was not baptized with the Holy Spirit upon his dramatic conversion, but received a few days later when Ananias visited him and laid hands on him specifically to be filled with the Holy Spirit (see Acts 9:17). Again, the biblical account does not directly say that Paul spoke in tongues upon his infilling, but we know he must have because later he gave testimony to the Corinthians, "I thank God that I speak in tongues more than all of you" (1 Corinthians 14:18).

How to Receive Holy Spirit Baptism

I really wanted to have a prayer language and tried so hard to sit in His presence and wait for it to happen. I was at youth group one night as a teenager and watched nearly everyone else around me receive and speak in tongues, but not me. I remember feeling that I was doing something wrong or that I was not spiritual enough. Fast forward many years later, and I remember waking up in the night groaning in my sleep while praying for my separated marriage, which was later reconciled. I opened my mouth and out bubbled the most beautiful utterance in tongues! I've never struggled since.

—Tonya Almenderez

People receive the baptism of the Holy Spirit in different ways. Some receive spontaneously and sovereignly without trying, others have hands laid on them to receive, and then others press into the blessing on their own and receive that way. There is no right or wrong way or even a right or wrong place to receive your heavenly language, just the promise that you will. If you, or someone you know, need to receive your supernatural language, here are some steps to help:

1. Believe in Jesus.

Sometimes people try to receive the baptism of the Holy Spirit, but they have not yet given their life to Christ. They do not receive Him because they have not met the internal conditions to do so. You have to be born again to receive the baptism of the Holy Spirit, but once you are, you do not have to wait to receive your prayer language either. You have the capacity right then and there to speak in other tongues.

2. Ask for it.

We see from the written word that we are encouraged to ask for the Holy Spirit. There is no qualifier for asking either, except that you be born again. You do not have to be perfect.

You do not have to have your life cleaned up. As eager as you are to receive, He is even more excited to gift you with your spiritual language. As a son or daughter of God, you do not need to beg either. Simply ask in faith and be ready to receive His glorious promise.

> "So I say to you: Ask and it will be given to you; seek and you will find; knock and the door will be opened to you. For everyone who asks receives; the one who seeks finds; and to the one who knocks, the door will be opened."
>
> Luke 11:9–10

3. Know that you will not receive something evil on accident.

Some people resist seeking the baptism of the Spirit because they fear they might receive a demon instead of the Holy Spirit. I can understand how some might think this way not yet knowing what to expect if they open themselves up to a spiritual experience. I want to assure you, however, that if you ask for the promise of the Spirit, then you will only receive the Holy Spirit, according to Jesus' words in Luke 11:11–13:

> "Which of you fathers, if your son asks for a fish, will give him a snake instead? Or if he asks for an egg, will give him a scorpion? If you then, though you are evil, know how to give good gifts to your children, how much more will your Father in heaven give the Holy Spirit to those who ask him!"

4. Speak in other tongues.

As I researched how other ministries teach on this subject, many propose that once you have asked for the Holy Spirit then you have automatically received the baptism and should be able to speak by faith in tongues right then and there in almost robotic fashion. Their approach to receiving the promise of the Spirit is based more in our legal and covenantal rights with God, while neglecting to mention the deeper relational components of the experience. Corey Russell, a senior leader at the International House of Prayer in Kansas City, wrote that speaking in tongues is a summons to experience the power of a Person—the Holy Spirit.[1] And Jesus refers to it as the "promise of the Father" (Acts 1:4 KJV) because it is deeply based in His Sonship.

Stepping into a new spiritual experience that is firmly grounded in relationship makes surrender much easier. When you ask the Father for the Holy Spirit, you then surrender your whole self, meaning your spirit man, your breath, your physical tongue, to allow Him to immerse you with His power until a glorious spirit language begins to flow from your innermost being.

Many people say their prayer language began with just one word or one syllable, and they spoke that out over and over until it developed into more sounds and even more words. Others have expressed that their spiritual language sounded like babbling at first, much like how a baby would sound, but it evolved over time into a more distinct language.

By the way, the Holy Spirit does not force you to speak in tongues. Instead, you give breath to the words that either bubble up or flow out from your spirit as you feel the infilling of His power. These are unpremeditated words that you speak out. They flow like a river from the inside of you, and once you have received your language, you do not lose it either.

As you engage this gift daily and it develops in you, there emerges a beautiful communion of words sealed in heavenly mystery between you and the Spirit of glory. This togetherness of words becomes the gateway to His manifest presence being seen through signs and wonders, wonders that all communicate He has come to dwell with us.

DIFFERENT NAMES USED FOR THE HOLY SPIRIT[2]

Holy Spirit (96 times)

Spirit of the Lord (28 times)

Spirit of God (26 times)

Eternal Spirit (Hebrews 9:14)

Helper (4 times by Jesus in John's Gospel)

Comforter (used throughout the Amplified Bible)

Holy One (Psalm 78:41)

The Lord (2 Corinthians 3:17)

Spirit of truth (4 times)

Spirit of Christ (Romans 8:9; 1 Peter 1:11)

Spirit of Jesus Christ (Philippians 1:19)

Spirit of counsel (Isaiah 11:2)

Spirit of knowledge (Isaiah 11:2)

Spirit of might (Isaiah 11:2)

Spirit of understanding (Isaiah 11:2)

Spirit of wisdom (Isaiah 11:2)

Spirit of the fear of the Lord (Isaiah 11:2)

Spirit of your Father (Matthew 10:20)

Spirit of glory (1 Peter 4:14)

Spirit of grace (Zechariah 12:10; Hebrews 10:29)

Spirit of judgment (Isaiah 4:4)

Spirit of burning (Isaiah 4:4)

Spirit of life (Romans 8:2)

Spirit of love (2 Timothy 1:7)

Spirit of power (2 Timothy 1:7)

Spirit of prophecy (Revelation 19:10)

Spirit of revelation (Ephesians 1:17)

Spirit of holiness (Romans 1:4)

Spirit of the Holy God (4 times in Daniel)

Notes

Chapter 1 What Is a Glory Carrier?

1. Bill Hamon, *Seventy Reasons for Speaking in Tongues: Your Own Built in Spiritual Dynamo* (Shippensburg, Penn.: Destiny Image, 2012), 70.

2. Guillermo Maldonado, *The Glory of God* (New Kensington, Penn.: Whitaker House, 2012), Kindle, chap. 1.

3. Ibid.

4. "Omni-," Merriam-Webster.com, https://www.merriam-webster.com/dictionary/omni-.

Chapter 2 Show Me Your Glory

1. "5457. phós," *Strong's Concordance*, Bible Hub, http://biblehub.com/greek/5457.htm.

2. I have heard this taught from different pulpits over the years but cannot remember who said it. Here are two links to support the suggestion, however: "Adam and Eve Clothed in Light Before the Fall: Origin of Teaching?," Christianity Stack Exchange, https://christianity.stackexchange.com/questions/47688/adam-and-eve-clothed-in-light-before-the-fall-origin-of-teaching; Ron Bateman, "Clothed in Glory," RevivalHut.com, September 10, 2017, http://revivalhut.com/clothed-in-glory/.

3. "5849. atar," *Strong's Concordance*, Bible Hub, http://biblehub.com/hebrew/5849.htm.

4. "Wholehearted," Merriam-Webster.com, https://www.merriam-webster.com/dictionary/wholehearted.

5. Phil Mason, *The Knowledge of the Heart: An Introduction to the Heart Journey* (Maricopa, Ariz.: XP Publishing, 2012), Kindle, chap. 5.

6. "H4872—Mosheh," *Strong's Hebrew Lexicon* (KJV), Blue Letter Bible, https://www.blueletterbible.org//lang/lexicon/lexicon.cfm?Strongs=H4872&t=KJV.

7. "H3115—Yowkebed," *Strong's Hebrew Lexicon* (KJV)," Blue Letter Bible, https://www.blueletterbible.org/lang/lexicon/lexicon.cfm?strongs=H3115&t=KJV.

8. Mike Campbell, "Reuel," Behind the Name, https://www.behindthename.com/name/reuel.

9. According to *Strong's*, worship (*proskyneó*) "has been (metaphorically) described as 'the kissing-ground' between believers (the Bride) and Christ (the heavenly Bridegroom). While this is true, 4352 (*proskyneó*) suggests the willingness to make all necessary physical gestures of obeisance" (reverence). "4352. proskuneó," *Strong's Concordance*, Bible Hub, https://biblehub.com/greek/4352.htm.

10. Maldonado, *The Glory of God*, Kindle, chap. 1.

11. Michael Lombardo, *Immersed in His Glory* (Shippensburg, Penn.: Destiny Image, 2018), 20.

12. Ibid., 22.

Chapter 3 The Shekinah Glory

1. Derek Prince, "The Laying on of Hands," *The Teaching Legacy of Derek Prince* XVI, no. 1, https://www.derekprince.org/Publisher/File.aspx?id=1000021532.

2. Tony Garland, "The Abiding Presence of God," *A Commentary on the Book of Revelation*, Bible Study Tools, http://www.biblestudytools.com/commentaries/revelation/related-topics/the-abiding-presence-of-god.html.

3. Ibid.

4. Bethel TV, "Glory Cloud @ Bethel," YouTube, December 19, 2011, https://www.youtube.com/watch?v=lvJMPccZR2Y.

5. Jeff Jansen, *The Furious Sound of Glory: Unleashing Heaven on Earth through a Supernatural Generation* (Shippensburg, Penn.: Destiny Image, 2017), Kindle, 48.

6. William D. Mounce, "John 1:14," *Mounce Reverse-Interlinear New Testament* (MOUNCE), BibleGateway, https://www.biblegateway.com/passage/?search=john+1%3A14&version=MOUNCE.

7. "What Were the 400 Years of Silence?," Got Questions Ministries, https://www.gotquestions.org/400-years-of-silence.html.

8. Eric Carpenter, "The Word Became Flesh and Tabernacled with Us," *A Pilgrim's Progress* (blog), http://eric-carpenter.blogspot.com/2009/12/word-became-flesh-and-tabernacled-with.html.

9. "G1544—*ekballō*," *Strong's Greek Lexicon* (KJV), Blue Letter Bible, https://www.blueletterbible.org/lang/Lexicon/Lexicon.cfm?strongs=G1544&t=KJV.

10. A. T. Robertson, "Mark 1:12," *Robertson's Word Pictures of the New Testament*, Bible Study Tools, https://www.biblestudytools.com/commentaries/robertsons-word-pictures/mark/mark-1-12.html.

11. "Jesus' favorite designation, in referring to Himself, was the 'Son of Man.' . . . Though the Bible does not define its exact meaning, the title 'Son of Man' probably refers to the fact that Jesus was perfect humanity." Don Stewart, "Why Did Jesus Call Himself the Son of Man?," Blue Letter Bible, https://www.blueletterbible.org/faq/don_stewart/don_stewart_793.cfm.

12. "G2853 – kollaō," *Strong's Greek Lexicon* (KJV), Blue Letter Bible, https://www.blueletterbible.org/lang/lexicon/lexicon.cfm?t=kjv&strongs=g2853.

Chapter 4 The Kabad Glory

1. To learn more about deliverance ministry, I recommend the books *Listen to Me, Satan!* by Carlos Annacondia (Charisma House, 2008) and *Free in Christ* by Pablo Bottari (Charisma House, 2000).

2. "Carlos Annacondia: The Evangelist at the Forefront of Revival," The Profile Interview, https://player.fm/series/series-2354532/carlos-annacondia-the-evange list-at-the-forefront-of-revival.

3. This summary comes from Carlos Annacondia's personal testimony at a few conferences, his book *Listen to Me, Satan!* (Charisma House, 2008) and a few web resources: Chantel Guajardo, "The Life of Carlos Annacondia," February 22, 2011, https://prezi.com/7bcqh6p9g1tt/the-life-of-carlos-annacondia/; Justin Brierley, "Carlos Annacondia: The Evangelist at the Forefront of Revival," *Premier Christianity*, https://www.premierchristianity.com/Past-Issues/2017/June-2017 /Carlos-Annacondia-The-evangelist-at-the-forefront-of-revival.

4. The Hebrew word *kabad* or *kabed*, when translated to English, has different spellings from resource to resource. To be consistent, I have chosen to spell it "kabad" unless I am quoting someone else.

5. "3513. כָּבַד(kabad or kabed)," *Strong's Concordance*, Bible Hub, http://biblehub.com/hebrew/strongs_3513.htm.

6. Ancient Hebrew Research Center, "Glory," Hebrew Word Definitions, http://www.ancient-hebrew.org/vocabulary_definitions_glory.html.

7. Maldonado, *The Glory of God*, Kindle, 98.

8. The most common biblical verses to support the phenomenon of being "slain in the Spirit" are Ezekiel 1:28; John 18:6; Acts 9:4; and Revelation 1:17.

9. John and Carol Arnott, *Preparing for the Glory: Getting Ready for the Next Wave of Holy Spirit Outpouring* (Shippensburg, Penn.: Destiny Image, 2018), Kindle, chap. 3.

Chapter 5 No Guts, No Glory

1. Wikipedia contributors, "Wagyl," *Wikipedia: The Free Encyclopedia*, https://en.wikipedia.org/wiki/Wagyl.

2. "Elizabeth Quay," ARM Architecture, http://armarchitecture.com.au /projects/elizabeth-quay/; "Perth Stadium's $54 Million Footbridge Revealed," *PerthNow*, June 6, 2015, https://www.perthnow.com.au/news/wa/perth-stadi ums-54-million-footbridge-revealed-ng-b9ce30d4908c71c2b3c0ecad7709136b.

3. "4436. puthón," *Strong's Concordance*, Bible Hub, http://biblehub.com /str/greek/4436.htm.

4. John MacArthur, "Stephen: The First Martyr," Grace to You, January 11, 2015, https://www.gty.org/library/sermons-library/44-24/stephen-the-first-martyr.

5. "The Grecians were Hellenists, or Jews who had imbibed the Greek culture, including language, of the countries in which they were born in the dispersion. They were considered inferior by the Hebrews, or Palestinian Jews, who were in

a majority in the church." Charles W. Carter and Ralph Earle, *The Acts of the Apostles* (Grand Rapids: Zondervan, 1973), 86–87.

6. MacArthur, "Stephen."

7. Leona Glidden Running, "Glory," *Ministry International Journal for Pastors*, February 1963, https://www.ministrymagazine.org/archive/1963/02/glory.

8. Maldonado, *The Glory of God*, Kindle, chap. 1.

9. Richard R. Melick Jr., "The Glory of God in the Synoptic Gospels, Acts, and the General Epistles," *The Glory of God Theology in Community*, eds. Christopher W. Morgan and Robert A. Peterson (Wheaton: Crossway, 2010), 80.

10. "Metamorphoo," *The NAS New Testament Greek Lexicon*, Bible Study Tools, https://www.biblestudytools.com/lexicons/greek/nas/metamorphoo.html.

11. "Time of the Transfiguration," *The Life of Our Lord upon the Earth*, Bible Study Tools, https://www.biblestudytools.com/classics/andrews-the-life-of-our-lord-upon-the-earth/part-iv/time-of-the-transfiguration.html.

12. Jennifer Eivaz, *The Intercessors Handbook: How to Pray with Boldness, Authority and Supernatural Power* (Minneapolis: Chosen, 2016), Kindle, 55–56.

13. Daniel and Amber Pierce, "The Reality of Israel Today: Embracing the Watchman Call!," Glory of Zion, August 18, 2014, http://www.gloryofzion.org/docs/8-18-14_PiercePrayerUpdate.pdf.

Chapter 6 I Will Not Go without Your Presence

1. Brandon Mercer, "San Francisco Bay Area Least 'Church Going' Metro In America," CBS SF Bay Area, August 28, 2015, http://sanfrancisco.cbslocal.com/2015/04/28/san-francisco-bay-area-least-church-going-metro-in-america/.

2. Lee Strobel, *Inside the Mind of Unchurched Harry and Mary: How to Reach Friends and Family Who Avoid God and the Church* (Grand Rapids: Zondervan, 1993).

3. Mark Mittelburg and Douglas Groothuis, "Pro and Con: The Seeker-Sensitive Church Movement," Christian Research Institute, http://www.equip.org/article/pro-and-con-the-seeker-sensitive-church-movement/; T. A. McMahon, "The Seeker-Friendly Way of Doing Church," The Berean Call, March 1, 2004, https://www.thebereancall.org/content/seeker-friendly-way-doing-church; Jeff VanGoethem, "The Seeker Service: Sentiment, Substance, and Symbol," Scofield Church, https://www.scofield.org/the-seeker-service-sentiment-substance-and-symbol/.

4. Bill Johnson, "The Value of Mystery," Bill Johnson Ministries, January 14, 2013, http://bjm.org/the-value-of-mystery/.

5. "Gnostics assert that matter is inherently evil and spirit is good. As a result of this presupposition, Gnostics believe anything done in the body, even the grossest sin, has no meaning because real life exists in the spirit realm only. Second, Gnostics claim to possess an elevated knowledge, a 'higher truth' known only to a certain few. Gnosticism comes from the Greek word *gnosis* which means 'to know.' Gnostics claim to possess a higher knowledge, not from the Bible, but acquired on some mystical higher plane of existence. Gnostics see themselves as a privileged class elevated above everybody else by their higher, deeper knowledge of God." "What Is Christian Gnosticism?," Got Questions Ministries, https://www.gotquestions.org/Christian-gnosticism.html. See also "Who Was Simon the Sorcerer?," Got

Questions Ministries, https://www.gotquestions.org/Simon-the-Sorcerer.html; Kaufmann Kohler and Samuel Krauss, "Simon Magus," Jewish Encyclopedia .com, http://www.jewishencyclopedia.com/articles/13747-simon-magus.

Chapter 7 Immersed in Glory Fire

1. Matthew Grant, "The Azusa Street Revival: It's Supernatural with Sid Roth," YouTube, January 1, 2015, https://www.youtube.com/watch?v=gxlsllcZNfI.

2. "What Does It Mean That God Is a Consuming Fire?," Got Questions Ministries, https://www.gotquestions.org/consuming-fire.html.

3. "907. baptizó," *Strong's Concordance*, Bible Hub, http://biblehub.com /greek/907.htm.

4. J. Hampton Keathley III, "Assurance of Eternal Security," Bible.org, June 30, 2004, https://bible.org/seriespage/assurance-eternal-security.

5. Sergio Scataglini, *The Fire of His Holiness: Prepare Yourself to Enter God's Presence* (Worldwide Publishing Group, 2014; currently published Minneapolis: Chosen), Kindle, chap. 14.

Chapter 8 Encounters with the Glory World

1. "The Wesleyans are an evangelical Protestant church group who trace their heritage back to John Wesley. Wesley was the founder of the Methodist movement, which came out of the Church of England in the mid-1700s." "Who Are the Wesleyans, and What Are the Beliefs of the Wesleyan Church?," Got Questions Ministries, https://www.gotquestions.org/Wesleyans.html.

2. Philip Richter, "Charismatic Mysticism," *The Nature of Religious Language: A Colloquium*, ed. Stanley E. Porter (Continuum International Publishing Group, 1996), 108.

3. Wikipedia contributors, "Holy laughter," *Wikipedia: The Free Encyclopedia*, https://en.wikipedia.org/wiki/Holy_laughter.

4. Kathie Walters, "Holy Laughter—What's It All About?," Sid Roth's It's Supernatural! and Messianic Vision, May 19, 2009, https://sidroth.org/articles /holy-laughter-whats-it-all-about/.

5. SacrificeOfPraise, "Joshua Mills—Arctic Miracles," YouTube, December 22, 2007, https://www.youtube.com/watch?time_continue=177&v=RV-mBHvjvy0.

6. Ruth Ward Heflin, "Glory," *Glory: Experiencing the Atmosphere of Heaven* (Hagerstown, Md.: McDougal Publishing, 1990).

7. Randal Luffman, "Silvania Machado, Testimony, Calvary Campground, Ashland VA," YouTube, July 20, 2014, https://www.youtube.com/watch?v=X Yq4nfuuDi4.

8. Ruth Ward Heflin, *River Glory* (Hagerstown, Md.: McDougal Publishing, 1999), Kindle, chap. 16.

9. Richard Stutzman, Facebook, https://www.facebook.com/richardstutzman /videos/vb.1483935390/10210152246231001/?type=2&theater.

10. Donna Grisham, "Hey Jennifer Eivaz I have experienced supernatural weight loss," Facebook, May 30, 2018, https://www.facebook.com/permalink .php?story_fbid=1982799105363493&id=100009002684036&__xts__%5B0%5D =68.ARAYNhCSKr0pHgEaOl8aWTddMbsAn5MLuToRvrhIyXhmUYYMrg4

RMEbny6hAnbGw59vIx1q-fwNg_HP5VP-Mqa6sa2mRVgwU_hwE7a8fDI4-5r
JxJ2f9-9INZaBRvrGVECXRHqA8YslSSqmo8_eCMJD3w70-WcjWSAReO8rp
k3nasVX9HcMHjQ&__tn__=-R.

11. Ibid.

12. ChristianPowerNow, "Gold Dust and Manna," YouTube, October 21, 2011, https://www.youtube.com/watch?v=fzG928yZQ1E; Jillene McKinney, "Dr. Harold Beyer Healed from Manna," YouTube, September 26, 2009, https://www.youtube.com/watch?v=sgSNCyRstnQ.

Appendix 1 Receiving Your Spiritual Language through Holy Spirit Baptism

1. Larry Sparks, "5 Ways That Praying in Tongues Will Change Your Life Forever," *Charisma Magazine*, March 20, 2014, https://www.charismamag.com/spirit/prayer/20030-5-ways-that-praying-in-tongues-will-change-your-life-forever.

2. This list is from *The Holy Spirit: An Introduction* by John Bevere and Addison Bevere (Palmer Lake, Colo.: Messenger International, 2013), chap. 1.

Jennifer Eivaz is a minister and international conference speaker who carries the wisdom and fire of the Holy Spirit. She presently serves as an executive pastor with Harvest Christian Center (HCC) in Turlock, California, and is passionate about teaching and activating the Body of Christ for intercession and hearing the voice of God. Jennifer's teaching style is authentic and aimed at the heart. She believes it is time for a balanced, biblical teaching on the gift of discerning of spirits, including how the gift is to be used and not used and how it is profitable, not only in the person's life who is gifted but in the lives of those around that person, and in cities and nations. Jennifer is a graduate of Oral Roberts University in Tulsa, Oklahoma. She is married to HCC's senior pastor, Ron Eivaz, and they have two children.

To find out more about Jennifer and her ministry, you can visit her online:

Website: www.jennifereivaz.com
YouTube: Jennifer Eivaz
Facebook: www.facebook.com/jennifereivaz/
Twitter, Periscope and Instagram: @PrayingProphet

Harvest Christian Center
225 Fourth Street
Turlock, CA 95380
www.harvestturlock.org

More Powerful Resources for the Spirit-Filled Believer by Jennifer Eivaz

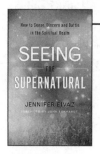